Your Outta Control Adopted Dog

Eve Adamson

T.F.H. Publications, Inc.
One TFH Plaza
Third and Union Avenues
Neptune City, NJ 07753

This book has been published with the intent to provide accurate and authoritative information in regard to the subject matter within. While every precaution has been taken in preparation of this book, the publisher and author assume no responsibility for errors or omissions. Neither is any liability assumed for damages resulting from the use of the information herein.

ISBN: 0-7938-2901-1

Printed and bound in USA

www.tfh.com

Contents

Help!
I've Adopted
a Monster!

In This Chapter You'll Learn:

* How your *dog's* history affects his present behavior

* How your *dog's* breed or mix of breeds affects his personality

* Characteristics of popular breeds

So, you've adopted a dog—congratulations! Whether you've found your dog at an animal shelter, adopted a dog from a breed rescue group, or taken in a stray, you've done something wonderful for another living thing. You've saved a dog from an uncertain existence or worse. But is it such a wonderful thing?

Many dogs from animal shelters are well-behaved pets who were trained and socialized as puppies. However, some simply didn't get the care and attention in their old home, and they may take a little extra work. If this sounds like your adopted dog, then this book is for you.

When your new little friend is eating your house, one bite at a time, refuses to acknowledge that the yard is supposed to be his bathroom, or

You couldn't resist that cute dog at the shelter—now it is up to you to make the relationship work.

barks and howls at the most inconvenient of times (or all the time), you might be thinking, "This isn't going to work. I'm going to have to take this monster back where he came from!"

Wait! When you wandered down the long hallway at the animal shelter peering at the dogs who barked, wiggled, blinked, or peered back at you, perhaps you got the feeling that one of them was for you. Maybe it was the cute wiggly one or the one who fixed you with a meaningful gaze, as if to say, "You know I'm yours, so let's just get on with it." Or maybe it was the one making all the noise. "She needs a buddy," you thought. "I can save her!"

Maybe you called a rescue group to get the purebred of your dreams, but now you realize somebody has taught your little one-year-old friend some awfully annoying habits. You did the research, you know this is the breed for you, or at least, you *thought* so...but then again, you didn't know Pugs shed this much; that Italian Greyhounds are this tough to housebreak; that Boxers were quite so strong; that St. Bernards would get to be quite so big so fast; that Bloodhounds were going to drool so

Rescue Operation

Purebred rescue organizations take in abandoned animals of a particular breed, whether found on the street, left with a vet or shelter, or surrendered directly to the rescue operation. Often run by devoted fanciers or breeders who have a lot of experience with the breed, rescue groups can be excellent places to find a purebred dog. Many of these dogs are adults who are already well trained, well mannered, and in desperate need of a new home. To find a purebred rescue group that specializes in your breed of interest, check out the American Kennel Club's (AKC) breed rescue page at http://www.akc.org/breeds/rescue.cfm. This website lists national rescue groups by breed. The national rescue coordinator can refer you to a rescue group nearest you, or call AKC customer service at 919-233-9767 and ask for specific rescue group information.

much; or that Great Danes were so incredibly needy.

The simple fact is that many people who adopt a dog from an animal shelter or a rescue group end up returning or abandoning that dog, especially when the shelter or group isn't practically fanatical about screening for the right match.

People fall in love with a dog, they adopt, they take their new friend home, and reality sets

You should take your family and living situation into consideration before adopting a dog.

Help! I've Adopted a Monster!

Can I Exchange This?

Remember that adopting a dog is not equivalent to buying a defective computer or a dress that fades the first time you wash it. A dog is a living creature, and a dog from an animal shelter or rescue organization has already been let down, probably more than once. Adopt with lots of research under your belt and do everything in your power to make the relationship work. Your dog deserves a good home and a human-for-life.

in. They try things that don't work and use training methods that aren't right for the dog or the human. They become desperate, then hopeless. And then, despite the guilt and regret, another dog is homeless yet again.

So, even if you think you've made a big mistake, even if you suspect you'll never be able to handle that barking, chewing, furry dynamo, don't give up just yet. Many adoptable dogs can make excellent pets, but they can't be expected to read your mind or even understand your words. They are dogs; they act like dogs. However, they are also smart and like to please you, so your job is to teach them and communicate with them about what you need them to do—and what you would much prefer they did not do—in a way they can understand. This book is here to help.

Who Recycled My Dog?

First, let's consider some of the reasons why a dog might be abandoned. Just because you adopt a dog that used to be somebody else's pet doesn't mean you are automatically adopting trouble. Sometimes, perfectly nice, even virtually perfect dogs are turned in to animal shelters and rescue groups. Some of the most common reasons why people abandon or relinquish their pets include:

Your Outta Control Adopted Dog

* A move to a place that doesn't allow dogs or makes life with dogs difficult (an apartment, a dorm, a condo, a place without a yard or fence, or having to travel overseas in a country with a canine quarantine, such as England);
* A life change such as marriage to someone who can't live with a dog, or divorce and a consequential move;
* A pet owner's death;
* An illness that makes caring for the dog impossible;
* A serious allergic reaction to a dog;
* A bad match between dog breed and human (such as a Border Collie adopted by someone who wants a dog to sit on the couch and relax all day);
* A rash adoption by someone not equipped to own a dog in the first place;
* A dog given as a gift to someone who didn't want or can't handle a dog;
* The dog engages in a behavior the people in the family can't tolerate and don't know how to correct.

Is it fair to the pets that they were given away? Of course not. Was it the pet's fault? Of course not. Not everyone is as devoted to their animal family members as you plan to be, and some people don't plan ahead when they buy a dog. In other cases, the owners are heartbroken about the relin-quishment, but don't have a choice.

Many perfectly sweet, trainable dogs are given up for adoption.

Help! I've Adopted a Monster!

Shiny Happy People

Most dogs, no matter how independent, would much rather have the people in their "pack" happy with them. A happy person means more treats, more petting, more enthusiastic utterances like, "What a good dog!" and even (dare we suggest it?) more chances to snuggle under the bedcovers at night. Happy people, from a dog's point of view, are a very good thing. If your dog knows how to make you happy, she'll do it, and do it gladly and willingly.

Behavior problems are among the most common reasons why people give up a dog, and sadly, most can be easily prevented. When a dog has a behavior humans don't like — it barks too much, "can't" be housetrained, chews the furniture, etc. — it's easy to blame the dog.

It's easy to think you just picked a "bad one," and that you can't do anything about it. In most cases, dogs who do these doggy behaviors aren't being bad, they are just being dogs. They simply aren't being properly managed by their humans. In other words, nobody told them, in a way they could understand, not to do those things and no one has told them that they have an option to do something right.

That's good news for you, the frustrated dog adopter. That means that chances are good your dog's "problems" are easily remedied with a little education, a lot of patience, and some regular training. The trick is communication. All you have to do is help your dog to understand the rules.

But how is your puppy supposed to know you don't like it when she barks? All that yelling you do just sounds like you're joining right in with her, barking at her side. If a swat should suddenly follow your "supportive" barking, well, that's just confusing. She may learn to distrust you, but she won't learn that you don't like barking.

Your Outta Control Adopted Dog

Worst Case Scenarios

In a few tragic cases, dogs have been so badly bred, unsocialized, and/or severely abused that they have behaviors that humans can't live with and that can't be fixed. Some dogs may be pathologically aggressive, so unsocialized that they refuse to trust humans, or have a disease that results in a high level of care impractical or impossible to the average pet owner. These dogs probably can't become good pets. However, shelter workers and rescue volunteers are trained to screen out these dogs and, in most cases, they won't even be offered for adoption. This is just one more reason why adopting a dog from a reputable rescue group or well-run shelter is so important.

The same goes for housetraining. If you rub your new dog's nose in his "mistake," he may well think some canine equivalent of, "Why the heck did she do that?" but he certainly won't extrapolate that odd and disturbing human behavior to mean that the lawn is a preferable potty spot.

No, you don't "speak" dog, just like your dog doesn't "speak" English (although he can learn to recognize many different words and associate behaviors with them). But there are many other ways to communicate with your dog, which we'll cover in detail in each chapter of this book.

How Breed Type Affects Behavior

Let's go back to that energetic Border Collie and his couch-potato human. Adopting a breed with behaviors that are incompatible with your lifestyle is a common scenario among impulse adopters. Bringing home a dog without considering the characteristics of the breed (even if you can only guess at them) can result in disaster. People see a cute puppy and they can't resist, but they do not do research on the breed's

Many shelter dogs have a hertitage that is a mixture of two or more breeds.

characteristics, and they find out too late that the dog is either too much or not enough for them.

Even if you've brought home a mixed breed, he probably resembles one or two pure-breds, and this can offer clues to your dog's behavior. Most animal shelters make an educated guess about what breed or breeds constitute the dogs they house. Many shelter dogs are mixes of just a few breeds, notably Labrador Retrievers, Beagles, Rottweilers, German Shepherds, and the ubiquitous random "terrier mix."

If your breed is a mix of a Lab and a German Shepherd, for example, he probably has a high energy level and is very strong and enthusiastic, but he may have a certain conservative attitude toward strangers. He may retrieve balls and try to herd the cat around the living room. A Beagle-terrier mix may be likely to follow a scent right into oncoming traffic and probably likes to bark a lot.

Knowing your breed will not only help you to pick a good match for your lifestyle, but it can also help you to solve problems you thought were unsolvable. When you understand why your dog barks, chews, jumps, or ignores your pleas to "Come," you will be in a better position to address the problem in a way that will work for your dog.

Your Outta Control Adopted Dog

The American Kennel Club (AKC) divides dogs into seven Groups or categories specifying the original purpose. Each group has lots of different breeds. For example, the Hound Group includes Beagles, Bloodhounds, Afghans, Basenjis, and Dachshunds—all very different, but with some important similarities.

The following will explain each group, the typical characteristics (remember that there are always exceptions), and some of the more popular breeds. Many hundreds of dog breeds exist, so these breed lists are by no means inclusive. For a complete list of breeds and their groups, visit the American Kennel Club website at www.akc.org. However, most dogs from animal shelters are a mix of the more popular breeds, and most of the breeds in breed rescue are also from popular breeds. (Rare breeds are less likely to be relinquished and, if they are, are usually snapped up quickly.)

Sporting Dogs

Sporting dogs are bred to be active and will need plenty of vigorous exercise. Sporting breeds are also keenly aware of the movements of small animals and birds, as they were bred to point, alert, and/or retrieve small game. Therefore, you may not be able to trust your sporting breed around small animals like gerbils or birds. Many sporting breeds can get along with cats, but it depends on the individual. Sporting breeds tend to be very tractable, which means they constantly look to you

Popular Sporting Breeds

Brittany
Chesapeake Bay
  Retriever
Cocker Spaniel
English Springer Spaniel
German Shorthaired
  Pointer
Golden Retriever
Irish Setter
Labrador Retriever
Vizsla
Weimeraner

Help! I've Adopted a Monster!

If your adopted dog is a member of the Sporting Group, he will require lots of exercise and activity to keep him healthy and happy.

to tell them what to do. They are very eager to please, so they tend to be easy to train. Training is a must, however, as many of these dogs are large and boisterous, with natural behaviors that can be destructive or dangerous. Your sporting breed craves attention from you and a clear communication of the "game" at hand, so training is rewarding for everyone.

Hounds

Hounds are independent hunters and independent thinkers who, although often can appear deaf to your wishes, are highly intelligent. Don't believe your Dachshund or Beagle is dumb. They just believe they have better things to do than to cater to the every whim of a capricious human. Unlike sporting breeds who look to their humans for direction, hounds are bred to get out there and hunt on their own. Hounds also

Your Outta Control Adopted Dog

Popular Hound Breeds

Hounds include both scenthounds (they hunt by tracking a scent) and sighthounds (they hunt based on their keen vision and fleet feet). Here are some favorites:

Scenthounds:
Basset Hound
Beagle
Bloodhound
Dachshund
Rhodesian Ridgeback

Sighthounds:
Afghan Hound
Basenji
Scottish Deerhound
Greyhound
Whippet

have a lot of energy and are so prey-focused that it can be extremely difficult to get them to come to you if they catch a scent or spy a squirrel. For this reason, hounds should never be trusted off-leash, especially in areas with traffic.

If your dog has any hound ancestors, he will be an intelligent but independent pet.

Popular Working Breeds

Akita
Alaskan Malamute
Bernese Mountain Dog
Boxer
Great Dane
Mastiff
Newfoundland
Rottweiler
Siberian Husky
St. Bernard

Working Dogs

Working dogs were bred to serve many purposes around the world, depending on where they originated. Many were all-around farmhands, pulling heavy loads, protecting livestock, and guarding property. These dogs had to be strong and healthy with weather-resistant coats and a protective instinct. Northern working breeds pulled sleds and were essential to travel and survival in the arctic.

Because of their heritage, working breeds tend to be exceptionally strong and require early training and socialization so that their humans (which they often outweigh) can handle them. They also tend to retain their protective, guardian instinct, so they must be responsibly managed. Working dogs are happiest when they have a job to do, even if it is simply pulling children on a sled, fetching the morning newspaper, or keeping squirrels out of the yard. They also tend to be exceptionally loyal and devoted to their humans.

Popular Terrier Breeds

Airedale Terrier
American Staffordshire
  Terrier
Cairn Terrier
Jack Russell Terrier
Miniature Schnauzer
Scottish Terrier
Soft Coated Wheaten
  Terrier
West Highland White
  Terrier

Terriers

These little balls of fire were created to keep vermin, such as rats, mice, possums, and weasels, out of the farmyard and fields. Their sharp barks and indomitable spirits make them challenging to

Your Outta Control Adopted Dog

Terriers can be tenacious and stubborn, but their compact size and determined spirit win them many admirers.

own, but their compact size makes them easy to handle. Terriers are awfully cute, but not everyone is cut out for life with these tenacious, stubborn, and vocal little dogs. When terriers get in a scuffle, they aren't likely to back down first. Terriers never give up. Tenacious to a fault, terriers are known to challenge dogs much larger and must be kept safe from their own egos. They can be taught to keep barking to a dull roar, but don't expect your terrier to be quiet all the time. They don't have it in their wild little hearts to be seen and not heard.

Toy Dogs

The toy breeds, as you can probably guess from the name, are lap-sized little fellows who love to play but whose primary purpose in life has always been to serve as human companions and sources of amusement. Adept at what they do, toy breeds love to keep their humans laughing with their silly antics, funny faces, and charming behaviors. They also love to snuggle, sit on laps, curl up on pillows, and generally live a life of luxury.

Help! I've Adopted a Monster!

Popular Toy Breeds

Cavalier King Charles
  Spaniel
Chihuahua
Maltese
Miniature Pinscher
Pomeranian
Pug
Shih Tzu
Toy Poodle
Yorkshire Terrier

Many toy breeds have been the pampered pets of royalty and the aristocracy all over the world, and while they retain their sense of privilege, most will be devoted to anyone who treats them well and offers them a comfy lap. They are easy to handle due to their size, but some can be quite demanding, and it's easy to spoil them. Remember that toy breeds are dogs, too, and should be trained, socialized, and held accountable for following the rules just like any other dog. Otherwise, you'll have a real little dictator on your hands—and in your lap.

Whether mixed breed or purebred, any puppy has the potential to become a loving companion.

Your Outta Control Adopted Dog

Non-Sporting Dogs

The non-sporting dogs are those that don't fit well into any other category, making this group hard to characterize. However, many of the non-sporting dogs would almost fit into other categories. The Chow Chow was a hunter and guardian. The Dalmatian has traditionally worked to clear the way for horse-drawn carriages, both of the gentry and, most

Popular Non-Sporting Breeds

Bichon Frise
Boston Terrier
Bulldog
Dalmatian
Lhasa Apso
Miniature Poodle
Schipperke
Shiba Inu
Standard Poodle

famously, for fire trucks. The Standard Poodle was originally a water retriever, and the Bichon Frise and Lhasa Apso look a lot like large toy dogs. Before adopting a non-sporting breed, make sure you do your research to find out what characteristics your breed of choice tends to have, so you can make sure you find the perfect match.

Herding Dogs

As the name implies, herding dogs were originally created to herd livestock on the farm. Herding dogs tend to be very driven and focused. They are highly intelligent and ready to learn any complex set of commands you want to teach them; however, they also have high-energy needs. If you don't challenge them, both physically and mentally, they will find a way to challenge themselves, often becoming destructive, escaping, or

Popular Herding Breeds

Australian Cattle Dog
Australian Shepherd
Border Collie
Collie
German Shepherd Dog
Old English Sheepdog
Pembroke and Cardigan
  Welsh Corgi
Shetland Sheepdog
  (Sheltie)

Help! I've Adopted a Monster!

Because herding dogs were originally bred to take care of livestock, they have a strong work ethic and energetic nature.

even developing neurotic behaviors that look a lot like human obsessive-compulsive disorders. Anyone who wants a highly interactive and active canine companion will do well with a herding dog, but don't expect members of this group to sit in a crate all day while you are away at the office and then be calm and relaxed when you get home.

Profile of an Adopted Dog

Let's consider Maya, an adopted dog. On a good day, her owner, Annette, describes her as "lively." Annette adopted Maya from an animal rescue group in Des Moines, Iowa, because she always admired Siberian Huskies and fell in love with Maya's happy energy and gorgeous, ice-blue eyes.

Annette is a preschool teacher, and at first she thought she would bring Maya to school to play with the children. After all, the school already

Your Outta Control Adopted Dog

had a resident Australian Shepherd mix named Izzy, who loved to retrieve pinecones and balls the kids threw to her, and a brand new black Labrador Retriever puppy named Otis, who, though he loved to steal backpacks and play keep-away, adored the kids and was good at snoozing on the front porch when it was required.

Right away, Annette realized that Maya was not going to be a good preschool mascot. Unlike Otis and Izzy who were

Every dog has a perfect owner waiting somewhere—make the right match from the beginning.

happily leash-free on the farm without incident, Maya is a Siberian Husky, which means, in the words of one Husky breeder I know, that "she will pull a sled from here to Alaska, whether you attach a sled or not." Although the preschool was far from the highway, it would take Maya only seconds to reach the road. She wasn't interested in four-year-old kids—she was too busy bounding through the cornfields.

Maya loved to play with the Lab puppy, but her extreme energy was hard to control. The first snow was like heaven to the young Husky, and she and Annette spent hours tramping through the fields, but this wasn't what Annette had envisioned. Living in a small apartment above the preschool without access to a fenced enclosure, she knew she would always have to be there, holding the other end of the leash, when Maya was outside.

Maya is a typical "outta control" adopted dog. Her good looks and sweet temperament got her a home, but her wild ways and classic Husky

Help! I've Adopted a Monster!

personality have made her a difficult pet for someone in Annette's situation. Luckily for Maya, Annette has lots of patience and has worked carefully to determine what Maya needs. After the disappointing revelation that Maya would never be a preschool-playground dog, Annette has come a long way in structuring an appropriate lifestyle for Maya and providing her with lots of socialization in settings that work, like long walks on a long leash, supervised time on a tie-out after the preschool children go home in the afternoon, play dates with Otis and Izzy, and more long walks on a long leash.

Abandoned Blue Bloods

According to Humane Society of the United States estimates, 25 percent of dogs in animal shelters are purebred dogs.

Maya is doing well, is happy to have such an understanding and loving human to care for her, and will probably calm down in another year or so, when her vigorous adolescence winds down. No, she won't ever be a couch potato, but with enough exercise and attention, Maya is shaping up to be a happy, healthy, and rewarding pet. Meanwhile, Annette is getting lots of exercise and is considering learning about skijoring, a fun sport made for dogs like Maya, in which a dog pulls a human through the snow on cross-country skis. Annette hopes she won't inadvertently wind up in Alaska.

Adolescence, aka Temporary Insanity

We all know humans go through adolescence, and it's no picnic. Anyone who has parented a teenager—in fact, anyone who remembers being a teen—has witnessed firsthand the extreme appetite, sleep needs, sense of rebellion, and hormonal surges, as well as the very extreme nature of the entire process.

Many dogs are relinquished to shelters during puppyhood and adolescence because owners do not understand that training, time, and guidance can remedy most outta control behaviors.

Dogs go through adolescence, too, but it doesn't take as long as humans, thank goodness. Unfortunately, many pet owners don't understand that dogs eventually grow out of this stage. Many thousands of dogs are relinquished to animal shelters during their adolescence because pet owners can't handle the behavior and believe it is permanent.

Adolescence in dogs can kick in anywhere from the middle to the end of the first year of life. Some dogs become quite mature at one year, and others take two or three years to settle into their adult state of mind and fully grown body.

Adolescent dogs have more energy than they will have when they reach mature adulthood. They may be more rebellious, sillier, and ganglier. They will probably challenge your authority now and then, breaking the

Help! I've Adopted a Monster!

Smells Like Teen Spirit

Adolescent dogs also may begin behaviors that make humans distinctly uncomfortable, such as lifting their legs on furniture and getting, shall we say, amorous with available human limbs. These sexual behaviors are more common in males. Neutering can help, but it may not completely resolve this behavior. Females who aren't yet spayed will also begin the menstrual cycle, which can be messy. Of course, spaying or neutering your pet before adolescence can prevent some of these problems.

rules they already know. I once had an adolescent Miniature Pinscher who, after I had been on the phone and ignoring him for what he thought was too long, climbed up on the back of the couch, looked me right in the eye, and urinated. "I'll teach you to ignore me," he seemed to be saying. "So there!"

Adolescent dogs may have mature bodies, but they are still puppies at heart.

Adolescent dogs are nearly full-grown in size, but still puppies at heart. They may seem unmanageably hyperactive and impossibly disobedient. They don't have full control over their gangly bodies or physical urges. Sound familiar, parents?

The good news is twofold. First, this, too, shall pass. By the age of two, or in some dogs that are slower to mature, by the age of three, your pet should settle down considerably, behaving

Your Outta Control Adopted Dog

much less like a super-kinetic, rocket-powered dog from hell and a lot more like the relaxed and happily lounging dog you had hoped would share the couch with you while you watch your must-see TV.

Second, even during adolescence, you don't have to give up and accept bad behavior. This is a time of intense energy, but also of intense learning. Lots of vigorous, fun, play-oriented training sessions, an obedience, agility, or flyball class, and fastidiously consistent house rules are crucial to make

Lots of exercise and training can help control teenage troubles in your dog.

adolescence bearable for all. If nothing else, make sure your active adolescent pet gets lots and lots of exercise. A couple of long, brisk walks each day should make a big difference in adolescent behavior. You know what they say—a tired dog is a good dog. As for housetraining mishaps and other lapses in behavior, you can always revert to rudimentary training you would use on a puppy, especially if your adolescent dog is acting like a puppy. Be kind, be firm, and don't take no for an answer. Avoid letting your dog get in situations where he can misbehave, but if it happens, quickly remove him from the situation, give him a time-out in his crate if he is being disruptive, and generally refuse to let your dog get away with things. He is testing you. It's up to you to pass the test.

When a Dog is Just Being a Dog

And sometimes, when all is said and done, your adopted dog is just being a dog. Mistaking dog behavior for bad behavior is a common

Don't Be Cruel

While dogs, especially adolescent dogs, require assertive handling and consistent enforcement of rules, they do not require corporal punishment. Hitting, slapping, or kicking a dog is never necessary. There is always a better way. No matter how frustrated your dog makes you, please preserve your relationship with your pet and avoid striking. This book will show you many ways to positively reinforce your dog's behavior and many ways to discipline your dog, but none of them include violence. Dogs may fear violent humans, but they don't understand them. When you use violence against an animal, you destroy communication.

mistake among first-time dog owners. People who have "been in dogs" for many years are more likely to accept that dogs bark, need things to chew, enjoy digging, and sometimes can't help themselves from jumping up to say hello.

If you are the sort of person who wants total control over the living creatures that share your house, perhaps you are better off with an aquarium. However, if you already have a dog, we hope you will be willing to live and learn, relax your standards to a reasonable degree, and summon whatever willpower you have to learn and maintain the important standards of good discipline, a comfortable routine for your dog, and lots and lots of love.

Why Does My Dog Do That?

In This Chapter You'll Learn:

✳ How to interpret common fear behaviors

✳ How to interpret aggressive behavior

✳ How to work with these behaviors

Anyone who has adopted a dog wonders about this new pet's mysterious past. Dogs from animal shelters were often picked up wandering, with no one to tell the shelter workers the dog's name, age, breed, or how it ended up on this country road or that busy intersection. Dogs from rescue groups may come with more information, but the people who give them up may not provide a complete or entirely accurate history.

So where did your dog come from? What were the real reasons she was surrendered? Why does she act the way she does? Why is she frightened of some things and obsessed with others? Short of consulting a pet psychic, what can you do to make life in your home easier for everyone?

Playing Sherlock Holmes

According to canine behaviorists, the first year of a dog's life is crucial for socialization and development. In fact, the first two to three months of life—the period before most people are even able to buy a puppy from a breeder—are particularly important. The experiences that puppies have may dramatically impact their personalities as adults. If a dog has mostly negative experiences with humans in the first year, it can be extremely hard and perhaps impossible to develop a trusting relationship later in life.

You may never discover how your dog ended up in a shelter or what his life was like before you adopted him.

When you adopt a dog, you will probably miss this developmental window, unless you pick up a box of abandoned newborn puppies on the side of the road. Your dog has been influenced by things you will probably never know anything about. However, your dog leaves clues to her secret past by the way she acts today. You can't ask your dog, "What the heck happened to you in that first year of life?" but you can pay attention to her behavior, reactions, and personality. You can learn a lot about your adopted dog just by watching her.

Fear Behaviors

Fear in dogs can be simple; for example, she doesn't like loud noises. They can also be complex; for example, she cannot function because of

Your Outta Control Adopted Dog

extreme shyness or anxiety, or people are in danger because she bites out of fear. While adopted dogs are vivacious and outgoing, some are fearful, and that fear can be the result of any number of complex interactions of genetics, personality, and life experience.

Unraveling the source of your dog's fear can be helpful when trying to solve behavior problems, but in many cases, you'll never know why your retriever mix quakes uncontrollably at the first rumble of thunder or why your small dog hightails it out of the room at the sight of any man but rushes to greet your girlfriends. What's most important is to determine the type of fear your dog is experiencing and to address it in a way that will help you and your dog to maintain a happy and safe relationship.

Quaking, Shaking, Shivering, and Crying

What's more pathetic than a dog quaking with fear at the slightest rumble of thunder, shivering with anxiety at the approach of a stranger, or whining and crying all night long when he can't sleep glued to your side? These involuntary physical responses to fear are common in dogs and a sure sign that your dog is afraid of something in his immediate environment. They can be clues to help you determine what exactly causes your dog to be afraid.

Many adopted dogs will display fears that can contribute to behavior problems. With training and patience, you can help your pet to overcome his fears and live a less stressful life.

Making Headway

If your dog is too submissive and fearful, avoid petting him on the head. Towering over your dog and bringing your hand down over his head, even as an affectionate gesture on your part, is an intimidating and dominant gesture in the mind of your fearful dog. To help build your dog's confidence and ensure him that you are his benevolent buddy, especially in situations where he is likely to submissively urinate or become particularly anxious, get down low and approach your dog from the side, not above. Pet him under his chin or on his forechest rather than on the top of his head.

Submissive Urination

Many fearful dogs are overly submissive when afraid and will urinate — all over shoes, the carpet, and the couch. My adopted dog, Sally, was housetrained from the day I brought her home from the animal shelter, but she submissively urinates whenever a man, such as my father or boyfriend, enters the house without me. My father takes it personally, but submissive urination is a natural behavior in dogs. Your dog is telling the source of fear—even if it is a person the dog knows and loves—"Yes, you are bigger and stronger, and I am definitely not challenging your authority!"

This kind of submission is helpful in a dog pack when, for self-preservation, a dog wants the top dog in the pack to know he isn't being challenged. It isn't so nice in a household, however. In general, your submissive urinator needs more self-confidence, but in particular, making less ado about the event that causes the urination can solve the problem. Whenever a man will be coming over to my house in my absence, I instruct him to completely ignore my dog upon arrival. When she isn't showered with attention from the intimidating semi-intruder,

Your Outta Control Adopted Dog

Overly submissive dogs may be easily scared or intimidated. Help build your pet's confidence by making your greetings less emotional and by showing him gentle affection.

Sally is just fine and is able to control her nervous bladder. Some dogs require more work than Sally when submissive urination is a serious problem. For these dogs, making less of an emotional event out of comings and goings can make a big difference, as dogs pick up on the emotions of humans, and an overly emotional hello or good-bye is likely to trigger submissive urination in dogs who are prone to it.

Fear Biting

Fear biting is a dangerous behavior in some dogs who are unsocialized or who feel cornered when faced with something fearful. If a small child backs a dog into a corner or the dog otherwise believes he can't escape, he may bite as a last resort. Some dogs bite before trying to flee, as a survival mechanism, even if their survival isn't actually at risk. You know your dog isn't in danger, but your dog doesn't. Dogs react out of instinct, and fear biting is a natural instinct in dogs.

Why Does My Dog Do That?

Many puppies were not taught bite inhibition, which can be dangerous, especially as they get older. Teach your young dog that biting is unacceptable in any situation.

However, in this world of lawsuits and in this country where dog bites have become almost an epidemic, fear biting is not an option. Any dog showing aggressive tendencies, whether they are motivated by too much self-confidence or not enough, is a potential liability to his owner, his victim, and himself.

Any breed of dog is a potential fear biter. The tendency to bite is based on the dog's feelings of security at the moment, his history of socialization, and whether he was taught bite inhibition (to refrain from biting human skin) at a young age, as well as other factors. Unfortunately, once a dog has seriously injured someone with a bite (or, depending on the victim, even if he has not seriously injured someone), you could be subject to a lawsuit, and a judge could decree that your dog be euthanized.

Your Outta Control Adopted Dog

Sometimes fear biting is something that just happens when a normally confident dog feels cornered, but if your dog is a regular fear biter, you need to get professional help immediately from an animal behaviorist or trainer specializing in this problem.

Fearful behaviors aren't good for anyone. Dogs who exhibit fearful behavior live lives filled with stress, which is mentally and physically draining. It may even compromise their immune systems

The Truth Bites

According to a 1996 study published by the Centers for Disease Control and Prevention (CDC) in Atlanta, Georgia, 4.7 million people are bitten by dogs every year in America, and 77 percent of dog bite victims are bitten by the family dog or the known dog of a friend. Over half of these dog bite victims are children.

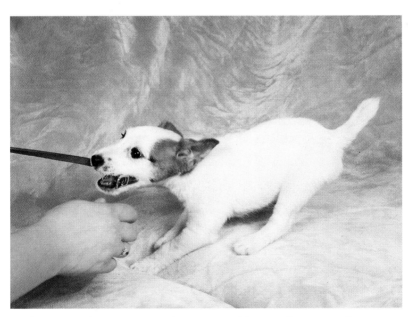

If your dog feels threatened or cornered, he may become a fear biter. For your safety and the safety of others, get professional training to help control your dog's aggression.

Why Does My Dog Do That?

and their health, not to mention their quality of life. Fearful dogs need help, and some fearful dogs need professional help from an animal behaviorist or a trainer specializing in fear behaviors.

The Causes of Fearful Behavior

Many different factors can contribute to fearful behavior in dogs, but most of them fall into one of the following categories.

Genetics

Some dogs seem to be congenitally fearful; even when raised with outgoing littermates under positive circumstances, they seem predisposed to shyness and caution. They may startle easily, act nervous, and be less likely than other littermates to barrel into a new situation. Some of these dogs are simply less outgoing than their siblings, just as some people are less outgoing than others. Yet, as with humans, a dog that is naturally fearful will live a life filled with stress. Life isn't fun when everything is frightening, and any minor change in routine represents a major source of anxiety.

Breeders who work carefully to breed dogs with good temperaments will avoid breeding dogs that are very shy, but unfortunately, there are breeders who don't consider temperament and will breed and sell any

Your Outta Control Adopted Dog

purebred dog. However, even responsible breeders will sometimes have a fearful puppy in a litter of potential champions. If you don't know your adopted dog's origins (and even if you do), you may never know if your dog's shyness or fear has a genetic component. However, if your adopted friend is generally well adjusted and happy when everything happens according to her normal routine but gets anxious by change and is generally cautious, she may simply have a shy personality.

Responsible breeders will carefully breed for good temperament; however, you may not know the origins or the parents of your adopted dog.

Your genetically shy dog needs special care and attention. She needs you to build her confidence through positive-based training and lots of rewarding experiences related to exposure to the outside world—other people, new places, other pets. Keep your dog safe as you gradually help her gain confidence. However, be forewarned that genetic shyness is extremely difficult to change. Your dog will probably always be shy, even if she learns to function acceptably.

If your dog is pathologically fearful due to genetics or any other reason, and this results in aggressive behavior, talk to your vet about your options. Aggressive dogs can often be helped and managed, but this is best handled by a professional. One mistake could result in severe liability for you, injury to someone else, and/or legally enforceable euthanasia for your dog.

Health Problems

Some dogs may be perfectly confident until they suffer health problems that make them weak, make them suffer pain, or compromise their senses. A blind or deaf dog can become easily startled by an approach they don't detect, which eventually leads to anxiety and a loss of confidence. Dogs who suffer from chronic pain may become more guarded, irritable, and prone to biting. Weakness can make dogs cautious and suspicious because they feel vulnerable. Many older dogs suffering from aging eyesight, hearing, or muscle weakness become more fearful. Older dogs can also suffer from a condition similar to Alzheimer's disease in which they become easily disoriented, confused, and forgetful, and eventually don't recognize things and people that were once familiar.

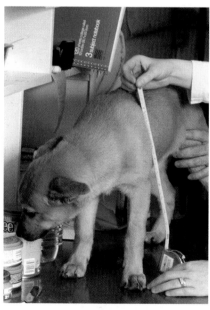

Make sure you take your adopted dog to the veterinarian as soon as you acquire him in order to get a clean bill of health.

Older dogs aren't the only dogs that can become fearful due to a health problem. Young puppies born deaf or with a painful condition or young adult dogs who develop a painful condition such as a ruptured spinal disk, early hip dysplasia, cancer, or heart disease may behave with extreme fear or even aggression. Until the health problem is diagnosed, it is difficult to know the source of fear. Always get a clean bill of health from your veterinarian before trying to address any behavior problems.

Improper or Absent Socialization

Just as you couldn't keep a child locked in a room for eight years then release him and expect him to function properly, neither can you neglect the socialization and training of a young dog if you want an adult dog that is friendly, confident, and secure. Socialization is the exposure of a young dog to many different people and situations during the first year of life. If a dog's experience is varied and his interaction with humans and other animals is usually positive, he will learn that humans and other dogs are good things and not to be feared.

However, dogs can easily become fearful if they spend their early lives homeless, have been stuck in breeding or pet store kennels without human interaction, or left in the backyard by their owners and not given a chance to develop relationships with other humans and dogs. As a survival mechanism, it makes good evolutionary sense to fear the unknown; however, an unsocialized dog is much more likely to bite out of fear, making him an unsafe companion for humans.

You can begin a slow, gentle socialization process with your adopted dog as soon as you bring her home. Just don't force her into situations that frighten her. Be patient, continue to build her confidence, take her with you

Proper socialization is essential for a well-adjusted healthy dog that is a productive member of society.

Old Dogs, New Tricks?

Is it too late to socialize a dog that wasn't well socialized in her first year of life? Maybe, but maybe not. It depends entirely on your dog's individual personality, genetic makeup, and health. It also depends on whether the lack of socialization included abuse and how well you handle the situation once you take her into your home. Many dogs that were unsocialized do learn to trust one or two people in their families, but may never be confident around strangers. Others—perhaps those with more natural self-confidence or an outgoing personality—learn to love and trust many humans, even if organized socialization doesn't occur until later in life. However, expect to put in a little extra effort to get there.

when you go out, and train her, with lots of praise and rewards, every single day. If your dog continues to be antisocial, she may always require more effort than a more confident and self-reliant dog. For many, the effort to socialize an unsocialized dog is well worth it.

Life's Ups and Downs

Sometimes, a perfectly happy and outgoing puppy can turn into a fearful dog due to life circumstances. A dog that thought he had a secure home and became very bonded to his family but was then relinquished to a shelter doesn't understand why his life has suddenly changed so dramatically. These dogs may be more prone to fearful behaviors.

Most dogs thrive on routines, and major life changes can be very stressful. Some dogs are more emotional than others and bond more intensely to humans. When they lose those humans, the result is often fear, anxiety, or even panic. They may bond even more intensely to their next owner.

Your Outta Control Adopted Dog

Some dogs are generally outgoing and may seem confident most of the time, but because of a particular frightening experience, they may fear certain sights or sounds. Many dogs fear thunder, fireworks, vacuum cleaners, or other loud sounds, even if they were never left outside in a storm or wandering on the fourth of July. Dogs have very sensitive hearing, so loud sounds are probably more stressful to them.

Your dog should look to you for guidance and discipline, as well as for cues on how to behave in certain situations.

In the most extreme circumstances, abuse by a human or an attack by another dog can drastically debilitate a dog's functioning. If your dog is so fearful that he quakes uncontrollably in any new situation or becomes panicked, foams at the mouth, even has seizures when exposed to something he fears, see a vet and ask about the temporary use of calming medications so your dog doesn't hurt himself. Then consider working with a canine behaviorist in order to address the extreme fear.

Ten Tips for Handling and Helping Fearful Dogs

No matter what the source of your dog's fear, there are some things you can do to help her gain confidence and courage. Try any or all of these tips and watch your dog conquer her fear, even if just a little bit at a time.

Why Does My Dog Do That?

Not the Newspaper!

Some dogs have a greater-than-average fear of certain stimuli—a rolled-up newspaper, a broom, the sight of dark-haired men, children, or certain kinds of dogs. My adopted dog, Sally, gets particularly anxious around Siberian Huskies. I'll probably never know why, but I can guess that perhaps she scuffled with a similar-looking dog, perhaps when she was on the run before being picked up by animal control. Dogs sensitive to particular fear triggers may have been abused or attacked. You will probably never know why, either, but be sensitive to your pet's particular fear triggers and try to avoid contact with them if possible.

* Give your dog a safe spot. Make sure she has a safe place like a comfortable crate to retreat to in times of stress. A crate or kennel is to your pet dog what a den is to a wild dog: a safe place to escape danger. It is a dog's best friend and can make her feel secure when she is anxious or afraid. A Nylabone® Fold-Away Pet Carrier can be set up or stashed in different parts of the house to offer your dog even more den options.

* Don't overreact. When your dog is nervous or afraid, you probably feel compelled to comfort her. A confident and gentle, "It's OK, Miss Foo," is fine, but overemotional coddling will reinforce the fear behavior. Don't let your dog think you are praising her for quaking, yelping, hiding, or submissively urinating.

* Set a good example. Dogs are very sensitive to the moods of humans. If storms make you nervous, you might be the source of your dog's anxiety more than the cracks of thunder. Don't make a big deal over things you know your dog fears, or you could make the problem worse.

* Be patient. Don't expect your adopted dog to conquer all her fears

Your Outta Control Adopted Dog

in a week of training. Some dogs may never be able to live fear-free, and others may take a while to gain considerable confidence. Be patient with your fearful dog, just as you would be with a person suffering from an anxiety or fear disorder.

✳ Make fear fun. No, the fear itself won't ever be fun for your dog. However, if you can transform a fearful situation into a fun situation, you can help your dog encounter it in the future—whether thunderstorm or approaching stranger—with slightly less trepidation and more expectation. If every time the fearful situation happens, such as a thunderstorm, you distract your dog with a fun reward, a treat, a game, a toy or something else pleasant, then thunder might eventually seem a lot less scary.

✳ Never stop socializing. Just because the first year of a dog's life is a crucial time for socialization doesn't mean socialization should stop after the first year. At least once a week, let your dog meet someone new and go to a new place. A dog that continues to experience new people and places throughout her lifetime with positive results (lots of praise, petting, and happy interaction) will continue to grow more confident and well-adjusted. She will be less likely to feel threatened and fearful in the face of change.

✳ Never stop training. Just because your dog finished a puppy kindergarten or basic obedience class

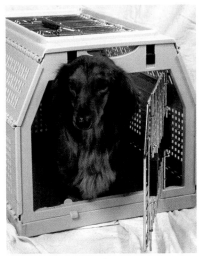

Give your dog a safe haven, like a Nylabone® Fold-Away Pet Carrier filled with a soft blanket and toys, so that he can retreat and relax if necessary.

doesn't mean your dog training duties are over. Train your dog for a few minutes every single day. There are always more things for your dog to learn—more tricks, more jobs, more good behaviors. Shy and fearful dogs benefit immensely from training. They get to be with you, they get to learn new things, and with every new learned behavior, they get lots of praise and rewards. What could be better for building confidence? If your dog is well behaved around the house, consider enrolling her in classes to learn advanced obedience work, agility, or Frisbee, or train her to earn her Canine Good Citizen® certificate. Let your dog work by carrying a dog pack on a hike or teaching him to fetch things for you. Let your dog succeed by building on each new skill.

✳ Don't get mad, get glad. When your dog submissively urinates, chews on something she shouldn't, or commits some other lapse in good behavior due to fear or lack of self-confidence, don't get mad. Anger and other forms of aggressive behavior only make fear and submission worse. We mistakenly believe that our dogs know what they did wrong because they look "guilty" when we return home and find a mess. Dogs aren't guilty; they are worried and fearful because in their past experience, when they are in a room with a human and a chewed shoe, bad things happen. They don't understand that you are yelling about something they did an hour before. Punishment doesn't work with dogs unless it happens at the moment of the infraction. If this situation occurs, greet your dog, clean up the mess without making a big deal about it, and work on ways to avoid the situation next time.

✳ Don't forget the vet. Remember, sometimes fearful behaviors are due to health problems. Make sure your dog gets a check-up every year and stays current on vaccinations. If your dog experiences a change in behavior or begins to act fearful for no apparent reason, have the vet give your adopted dog a health clearance before looking at other factors.

Your Outta Control Adopted Dog

✳ Be fair. Most importantly, your dog looks to you to be a fair and benevolent leader. Never punish your dog in anger, be sure your dog understands the problem so she continues to trust you, and don't destroy your relationship with yelling and hitting. Your dog doesn't require a smack; she requires leadership. She needs you to show her what she can and can't do, just like a small child. Kids with firm, kind, and consistent parents are likely to grow up to be self-confident, self-disciplined, and well-adjusted. You can give that gift to your dog, even if she never lived under benevolent leadership before. Teach her that some humans know how to behave and that she doesn't have to be afraid any more.

Aggressive Behaviors

While some adopted dogs are fearful and insecure because of their experiences, many become aggressive. You may never know if aggression was the reason for a dog's surrender, although most shelters and rescue groups try to screen out aggressive dogs. Not all aggressive dogs are beyond help. Many have simply never been taught that a human is now in control.

Aggression can be genetic, and when it is a matter of temperament, it can be a tough situation. Some genetically aggressive dogs will never make good pets. When aggression stems from circumstances, it may be a situation you can remedy with the help of a professional trainer or, in severe cases, a trained animal behaviorist.

Some dogs—like some people—are simply more aggressive than others. Some dogs transform from confident to overconfident under certain circumstances. Some breeds tend to be more assertive, but breed is only peripherally related to this tendency. Any dog of any breed can have an aggressive personality, although some working breeds with a history of guarding may be more likely to behave in an aggressive manner.

Even the tiniest dog can be a real dictator if you let him think he is master of the household. Of course, when a small dog is aggressive, he isn't as dangerous to humans as when a large, strong breed becomes aggressive. It's simply an issue of size. Let's look at the size/breed issue for a moment.

Big Dog, Big Trouble?

Some breeds become aggressive because during that first crucial year of socialization, no human ever took charge or taught them that they need to follow human rules. Perhaps they weren't taught bite inhibition, weren't made to work for their meals, or had owners who acted intimidated around them. Worse yet is when dogs are allowed to roam free in groups. Dogs often operate on instinct, and when two or more dogs are gathered together, leash-free, without the proper training and supervision, a pack mentality can set in. Any small quick movement can trigger the pack's prey instinct, and they can attack. A pet Rottweiler who has been well socialized and well trained by humans can be the most loving, loyal, and gentle of pets, a supreme babysitter, and devoted

Some breeds may be inherently more assertive than others, but aggressive behavior must be properly managed in any dog, no matter the size.

Your Outta Control Adopted Dog

family member. Consider the Rottweiler in the news a few years back that followed the family's four-year-old child into the woods and kept him warm and alive on a cold winter night when the child couldn't find his way back home. However, a pack of unsocialized and untrained Rottweilers (or any dogs, including mixed breeds—I certainly don't mean to pick on Rotties) roaming free in the countryside could encounter a small child, a small dog, or a calf, and you would have a completely different—and often tragic—result.

Often, dog aggression is a result of poor management by humans. Some people shouldn't have dogs, period. Some people don't have the right personality to manage an overconfident dog. Consider all the stories of dog attacks in the news in the past few years; most of these were examples of poor human management. Large dogs are a big responsibility, and you can't just adopt one and expect it to behave all on its own.

Owning a large dog is a big responsibility. Proper training and socialization is essential.

Why Does My Dog Do That?

However, not all aggression results in tragedy, and not all large dogs or members of certain breeds are overconfident. Some are fearful and insecure. Some are emotional and needy. Some are great big babies in big-dog bodies.

Adopting a large dog does come with a very serious responsibility. You can't manhandle your dog into behaving, so you must train, socialize, manage, and be responsible for him. Showing society how well-behaved, sweet, confident, and obedient these large dogs can be takes work, but you'll have one of the most devoted and loyal companions you can imagine.

How Submissive Are You?

Aggression is completely different than healthy self-confidence. A healthy, well-adjusted dog is confident enough to enjoy life but knows who is in charge and doesn't challenge the "pack" leader's authority. An overly confident dog (and this isn't all that common) might challenge your authority. More common is a human who behaves in a way that sends the dog message, "I'm part of the pack, but you rule my behavior." Confident dogs feel compelled, in such situations, to step in and take the role (somebody has to do it!) of pack leader. A dog that

Tug-of-War: Do or Don't?

It may not a good idea to play tug-of-war or other rough games with your large dog, who can probably out-tug, out-run, and even out-wrestle you. When you "lose" these games, it sends a message to your dog that he is dominant over you. On the other hand, letting a shy, fearful, smaller dog win an occasional gentle game of tug-of-war or keep-away can help build confidence. Some studies refute the connection between tug-of-war and dominant behavior.

Your Outta Control Adopted Dog

"corrects" your behavior probably sees himself as your superior, and you may have been leading him along with inadvertent clues.

If your adopted dog had an owner who acted submissively, he may be in the habit of lording it over humans. That doesn't mean you can't show him that in this household, things are different. But first, make sure you aren't showing your dog signs of submission, such as:

* Feeding your dog without making him sit or lie down first;
* Giving your dog treats without making him first do something to earn them;
* Feeding him before you eat your dinner;
* Petting him every time he tries to get you to pet him;
* Letting him push through doors in front of you;
* Not responding, acting fearful, or backing away when your dog growls or snaps at you;
* Losing a game of tug-of-war with your dog;
* Yelling at your dog (it sounds like barking);
* Whining at your dog (it sounds like you are a whining littermate);
* Averting your eyes first (eye contact and holding the gaze longer is a dominant behavior).

That being said, some behaviorists and trainers argue that you can't out-dog a dog. That means that playing the dominance game your dog's way is a losing proposition. It's one thing not to act submissive—that's important. It's another thing to try to outdominate your dominant dog the way another dog would.

You aren't a dog. Dogs have many advantages over us, and you can't compete in the world of dogdom. However, you are a human and have many advantages over a dog. The way to dominate your dog is by not playing his game.

Why Does My Dog Do That?

You don't have to physically dominate your dog, but you must mentally dominate your dog. Your dog should respect and adore you. If he would do anything to please you and gain your respect, you've got it made. How do you do that? Even with an adopted dog who thinks he rules the human race, you can gradually alter his world view. Try the following tips, and never back down. As soon as your ultra-confident dog senses a weak spot, a tendency to give in, he'll go for it. (Ever met a toddler? Then you know what I mean.)

❋ Never give your dog anything good without making him do something for it first. He wants a treat? Make him lie down and stay for one minute. He wants dinner? Make him wait until you are done eating, then sit and wait until you put the bowl down and give the release command. Better yet, hand feed your dog his meals, making sure he takes the food from you gently. He wants a toy? Make him roll over, shake, or retrieve something first. A dog that gets a free ride thinks he deserves a free ride. A dog that has to

Dog City

The more dogs that are in a household, the more behavioral problems, and the more likely the owners are to surrender those dogs to shelters. Ideally, you should get one dog at a time, with a year in between to be sure each dog gets enough individual attention, socialization, and training to be able to bond with you and learn the rules. More dogs makes it harder to enforce rules, and owners are less likely to spend as much time with their pets, reasoning that the dogs have each other. Be realistic about how many pets you can afford and how many pets you have time to take care of responsibly. You might think twice about going back to adopt another dog...just yet.

Hand feeding your dog treats will teach him to be gentle and to respect his family members.

work for a living appreciates what he has, as well as the person who doles it out.

* Don't let your dog drag you down the street by the leash. Who's walking whom, anyway? Stand like a stone and don't move until he stops pulling. Walk, and when he walks nicely, praise; every time he starts pulling, stop. Don't move until he stops pulling. Boring? Sure, but your dog thinks so, too. He wants to get going. Show him that the only way he's going anywhere is to quit yanking you along.

* Don't give your dog anything if he is jumping on you to get to it— not an ear scratch, not even eye contact. Give him the verbal command to sit or lie down nicely before giving him what he wants. No exceptions!

* Don't let your overly dominant dog sleep on your bed or on any furniture unless it is specifically designated for dogs and something that you don't use. Eventually, when your dog is under better control, you may be able to relax this rule, but immediately

Why Does My Dog Do That?

revoke furniture privileges (and especially bed privileges) if your dog starts to rebel again.

✳ If your dog pushes past you through a door, call him back and make him sit. Go through the door, then call him through after you—every time!

Handling Aggression Safely

It can be difficult for a novice pet owner to tell the difference between a dog whose aggression is manageable and a dog whose aggression is a danger to itself and others. Animals are unpredictable, and adopted dogs with unknown pasts can pose a real puzzle to those who love and train them. However, many dog trainers and animal behaviorists specialize in aggression, as it is such a common concern among dog owners.

An animal behaviorist or a trainer that specializes in management problems can help you learn how to communicate with your adopted dog.

Your Outta Control Adopted Dog

Who to Call: Trainer or Behaviorist?

While many animal behaviorists are also dog trainers and some dog trainers become animal behaviorists, there is an important difference between these two professions. Your particular problem determines whom you should call. An animal behaviorist is a person that specializes

Help for Owners

A few sources for finding trainers and behaviorists are the following:

Association of Pet Dog Trainers

17000 Commerce Parkway
Suite C
Mt. Laurel, NJ 08054
www.apdt.com/
1-800-PET-DOGS
This group is a large and reputable organization of dog trainers committed to positive and non-abusive training methods. They have a section on their website about how to choose a trainer, and a search engine to find member trainers in your area.

Association of Companion Animal Behavior Counselors

c/o American Institute for Animal Science, Inc.
PO Box 7922
Rego Park, NY 11374-7922
www.animalbehaviorcounselors.org/
This organization has a "Find a Certified Counselor" search engine on their website.

Animal Behavior Society

Indiana University
2611 East 10th Street #170
Bloomington, IN 47408-2603
www.animalbehavior.org

in animal behavior problems, sort of like an animal therapist. Certified animal behaviorists have advanced degrees and are trained to uncover the root of abnormal behavioral problems like extreme aggression, debilitating anxiety, and obsessive-compulsive disorders, and address solutions for them. Dog trainers can also be certified, but serve an important yet different function. Trainers address pet management problems—those doggy things that are normal for dogs but that humans don't like—by training your dog. They also train you to better communicate and help you with techniques and management strategies for a successful relationship.

The gratitude and devotion that adopted dogs shower their owners is worth the time and work you put into the relationship.

Your Outta Control Adopted Dog

Addressing your concerns with a responsible professional is worth every penny, so please consider hiring a specialist if you are at all concerned about aggression in your dog.

Gratitude: The Big Payoff

In my opinion, one of the very best things about adopted dogs is the gratitude so many of them seem to have toward the humans who adopted them. Hundreds of people who have adopted dogs have told me over the years that the dogs bonded strongly with them, and they developed an intense and special relationship.

Your dog's version of gratitude may result in a Velcro dog that never leaves your side, a happy-go-lucky, confident dog who always keeps one eye on where you are and will do anything to please you, or even an overconfident dog who becomes forever loyal and fiercely devoted to you.

Whichever profile best fits your adopted dog, you've got a friend for life, and that's one great big payoff for all your hard work.

Your Adopted Dog's Best Influence

By now, you should know or be able to guess your dog's breed or mix of breeds, and you have determined what characteristics tend to go with that type of dog. You also know what some of your dog's problems and issues are. You may even know, or at least suspect, where those behaviors originated.

Now you have your dog and are committed to sticking with her and preserving the promise you made when you adopted her, it's time to take all that information and do something with it. It's time to start building the foundation of your relationship.

You and Your Buddy

Even if you've had your adopted dog for months or years, you can start over and reset your own behaviors, which will in turn reset your adopted dog's behaviors. One thing many pet owners don't realize is that when dogs misbehave, it is usually a matter of a human's failure to communicate. While I don't mean to make dogs sound like computers, behavioral problems are largely a matter of user error.

In theory, your dog wants to please you. Yet, if he doesn't know how, or something else is more tempting, rewarding, delicious, or chaseable, then you may find yourself losing the battle for your dog's attention. But you can help your dog to want to please you, as well as to know how to please you, most of the time. (Hey, nobody's perfect, and as I said, dogs aren't computers.)

The most important thing you can do for your dog is to teach him how to adjust to life in his new home and how to get along with your family.

The most important thing you can do to help your adopted dog adjust to life in your household is to forge a relationship. That relationship will be the basis for everything else you do, and the trust it involves will be the basis for your dog's desire to please you. It will also help you to be more understanding when your dog acts like, well...a dog, occasionally making a mistake, getting distracted, nibbling on the Thanksgiving turkey, or waiting a few too many maddening seconds before coming when called.

How Do We Love Dogs?
Let Us Count the Ways...

According to a 1999 survey by the American Pet Association:

✳ 41 percent of American pet owners display a picture of their pet in the home

✳ 17 percent of owners keep a picture of their pet in their wallet

✳ 9,843,962 dog owners celebrate their dogs' birthdays

✳ 28,539,216 dog owners purchase Christmas gifts for their dogs

✳ 10,100,000 dogs in America sleep on the bed with their humans

When you and your dog have forged a relationship, you have a friendship. Sure, it's an inter-species friendship, but it is a friendship nevertheless. Sometimes that friendship will seem more like a parent-child relationship and sometimes more like a teacher-student relationship, but it remains a relationship. You will (and probably already do) have a connection. Your valuable relationship will be worth preserving and will give you even more of a reason to work through your challenges.

But how do you build a relationship with your dog? It's simple, and this chapter will show you how.

Assessing Your Adopted Dog's World View

Every dog is different. Sure, all German Shepherds have similar characteristics, as do all Yorkshire Terriers, Afghan Hounds, and Chesapeake Bay Retrievers. Yet, every dog has a unique and individual personality.

Four Legs are Better Than Two

According to the American Pet Association, more than half of American dog owners report that they are more attached to their dogs than to their best friends, children, or spouses.

Getting to know a dog is a lot like getting to know a human friend; some are optimistic and cheerful; some are quiet and laid-back; some are energetic; some live to veg-out on the couch; and some are so perky that only perky humans can stand them.

You can't just program your dog to have a particular personality. Your Malamute can learn to sit and stay, but he might not ever enjoy playing Frisbee. Your Pekingese can learn to sit still for grooming, but he may never condescend to acknowledge the cat. Your Miniature Pinscher might grudgingly wait for you to finish dinner before asking

Your dog has a unique and individual personality—the fun part is getting to know him and becoming friends with him.

Your Outta Control Adopted Dog

for his, but he probably won't ever be a laid-back, go-with-the-flow kind of dog, just as your Bassett Hound may never get very excited about anything, no matter how much you jump up and down and implore him to get a little enthusiastic. Then again, that same Bassett Hound's sister may be as jubilant as the jolliest of Jack Russell Terriers, even if you encourage her to please, please, please just sit on the couch and relax.

It's all a matter of personality.

In many happy instances, a dog and his human have complementary personalities. You're quiet, but your funny little Pug cheers you up and brings you out. You get stressed out and anxious, but your rock-steady Bernese Mountain Dog helps calm you down. It can be just as nice when your personalities are congruous. You like to get up and go and so does your bubbly Cairn Terrier. You like to lounge in bed all morning and so does your elegantly mellow Whippet.

However, problems can arise when you have a personality clash. While you can reduce the possibility of this happening by getting a breed that tends to have a temperament suitable for your lifestyle, you never know about personality. A woman I once interviewed had carefully researched many breeds and chosen a Welsh Springer Spaniel because of

With careful research, you can pick a dog that fits in perfectly with your personality and lifestyle.

Your Adopted Dog's Best Influence

Two Dogs, Half the Bonding

Many people believe that two dogs are better than one. In many ways, they are, especially if you aren't home very often. Two dogs offer each other companionship and a playmate. However, if you adopt two dogs at one time, it can be very difficult to find the time to bond fully with both dogs, and they will be more likely to bond to each other and less strongly to you. Better to adopt one dog, bond with it and train it for a year, and then bring another dog into the family when your first dog is well trained and attached to you.

Your adopted dog can help introduce you to new experiences. This Lab/Golden mix is a guide dog.

their happy but mellow personalities. Her first dog fit her requirements precisely, and he was a perfect match. When she decided to get a second Welsh Springer Spaniel, however, she got a much livelier and more active dog. While the two Welshie "sisters" adore each other, their bewildered human swears that these two dogs, both from a wonderful and reputable breeder, couldn't possibly be the same breed.

So what happens when your adopted dog foils your expectations and turns out to have a personality that you didn't expect? Well, life is full of surprises, isn't it! Parents sometimes have the same problem with their children. Laid-back parents get an extremely talkative or hyperactive child, or highly active, athletic parents get a child who would rather read or play the violin. Of course, you can't trade in your child for a different one. These parents make do, ideally allowing this new, challenging little personality to expand their horizons, open them to new experiences, and help them to learn patience, tolerance, and appreciation for someone who is most certainly unlike themselves.

You can do the same with your dog.

Bonding with Your Adopted Dog

The first step in working out your relationship with your dog is to get to know and like each other. Young puppies usually bond quickly with people, and many older adopted dogs that have already lived with other humans will also bond quickly with any humans who treat them well.

Some dogs may take longer to bond with you, especially if they were very attached to their previous owners, have lost trust in humans, or are simply more cautious. Some breeds are more likely to bond with a new human quickly, and others take longer. For example, a Boxer rescue person once told me that Boxer rescue was less stressful

Consistency, a regular schedule, and lots of attention and affection will help your dog bond with you more quickly.

because Boxers adore whoever is kind to them. A week later, a St. Bernard rescue person told me that Saint Bernards become very bonded to their people and often get depressed and mournful for quite awhile after being abandoned. They consequently bond even more strongly to the person who rescues them.

Any member of any breed is potentially sensitive to losing its previous humans. Much depends on individual personality as well as the circumstances of the loss. Dogs that have a hard time with adoption may take some patience—and probably won't be available for regular adoption at your local animal shelter. You may work with a purebred rescue group to find a dog like this; however, be willing to spend lots of time cultivating that relationship.

Try not to be disappointed if your dog doesn't take to you right away. Consistency, a regular schedule, a soft voice, and gentle affection will eventually win over your cautious new friend. When your adopted dog learns that she can trust you to keep her safe and well fed, and that you

Health Watch

In some cases, a dog may fail to bond with humans due to pain or illness. Be sure your adopted dog has been checked by your vet, and if your dog continues to have problems relating to humans, ask your vet if any additional examination or tests might be helpful. Describe your dog's behavior carefully and note any unusual behaviors to your vet, such as increase in or loss of appetite, lethargy, fatigue, seizures, startling, or anything else that seems strange to you. Knowing how your dog behaves can help your vet to diagnose any underlying health problems.

Your Outta Control Adopted Dog

are consistently available to pay attention to her and play with her, she will open up to you.

In most cases, an adopted dog will probably bond with you fairly quickly. However, the slow and steady building of a positive relationship between dog and human is a long-term process. If you spend quality time with your adopted dog every single day—and that includes games of fetch, snuggle sessions on the living room floor, and training sessions—your dog will learn to enjoy and anticipate your company and trust you. He will

If you spend time with your dog every day, he will soon learn to trust and depend on you.

also consider you part of his pack and will do what he can to protect you (even from dust bunnies), warn you of intruders (even if the intruder is a squirrel), and help you in any way that you let him.

Your dog doesn't mind if all you do together is hang around on the couch, but there are many different ways you can spend time with your dog that will allow you to cultivate your relationship and get to know each other. Here are some ideas:

❋ Go on exploration walks. Instead of the same walk around the block every day, take different paths and discover new sights, sounds, and smells together.

❋ Play a game, just for fun, for five to ten minutes every day. Try fetch with a ball, rope, or Frisbee, or play tag or chase.

Your Adopted Dog's Best Influence

Travel Safety

When you take your dog along in the car, be safe. Buckle your dog into a dog seatbelt or put him in a strapped-in crate to keep him and other passengers safe in the event of a car accident. Also, never leave your dog in the car on a warm or sunny day. A car can heat up quickly, just like a greenhouse, and many pets die each year from being left in parked cars in the heat.

* Whenever you go out in the car, take your dog if possible. Dogs love to go for car rides, on errands around town, or on day trips. My dog Sally loves to go through the drive-through at the bank and the pharmacy because they always have a jar of dog treats at the window, and of course, what dog doesn't enjoy an occasional foray through the fast food drive-thru? (And what indulgent pet owner doesn't occasionally order that additional plain hamburger with no bun?)

* Tell your dog about your day. Whether she understands or not, she'll be happy to listen to you. Dogs are very tuned-in to the feelings of their humans. They are happy to join in celebration of a good day and are expert comfort-givers after a bad day.

* Going outside to get the mail? Pick up the newspaper? Pull weeds? Chat with the neighbor? Don't leave your dog inside, peering out the window. Take him out there with you.

* After basic obedience, take a specialized class to learn competitive obedience, agility, Flyball, competitive Frisbee, or any other dog activity available in your area.

* This one sounds obvious, but it may not be so obvious: Make sure the time your dog spends with you is actually fun. Speak nicely to your dog, pet her, give her treats, have a good time. The more rewarding it is to be with you, the more bonded she will become.

Teaching and Re-Teaching Good Habits

Uncovering what your dog does and doesn't know when you adopt him can be a bit of a puzzle, but chances are, your dog knows at least a few things. Maybe your adopted dog is mostly housetrained, knows "sit" but not "down," and starts out knowing not to beg at the table until your three year old makes it just too rewarding not to linger under the highchair acting as resident vacuum cleaner.

Part of adopting a dog is the continual teaching—and re-teaching—of good habits. Your dog may not be a puppy anymore, but contrary to the old saying, you can teach your old dog new tricks, and you can teach, or re-teach, good behavior. If your dog lived with a family before, he probably knows, or at least suspects, that he shouldn't use the house as his toilet or steal food off the table. However, he may not know that he shouldn't jump on people or bark incessantly for an hour. It is your job, as your adopted dog's new guardian, to keep control of his behavior.

Your dog may not be comfortable in your home right away; you must teach him the rules and be consistent when enforcing them.

Puppy Litter Box?

Many people with very small dogs aren't able to take their pets outside for walks or potty breaks easily. Dog litter, a relatively new invention, can be the perfect solution for these pets. They can relieve themselves in the home in a litter box filled with paper-based pellets that absorb liquid and odor, which is easy to clean up. Training your dog to use litter boxes depends largely on your individual dog, but many toy dogs never "go" anywhere else. Dog litter boxes come with complete instructions on use and training, but training is similar to any other housetraining method.

Don't relent; don't let up; and don't let him get away with it, or he'll learn that he can get away with it.

The challenge of this kind of relentless re-teaching is that it takes time. You can't just adopt a dog and leave it alone if you want a well-behaved family member. However, if you invest a serious amount of time in the first few months to your adopted friend, you will have a well-behaved dog for life. If you aren't willing to put in that time, you shouldn't adopt a dog! If you have already adopted a dog, then please do what is best; rearrange your schedule a bit and make the effort and the commitment to show your dog how to behave in a gentle, loving, positive, but firm, assertive, and flawlessly consistent manner. You must show your dog how to behave. Just remember, your dog wants to learn. It's all about communication.

The Importance of Routine

No matter how spontaneous your exuberant adopted dog may seem to be, all dogs thrive on a regular routine to bring out their best. Dogs like lives of regularity. They like to eat at the same times every day, go to bed at the

Your Outta Control Adopted Dog

same time every day, and play, train, and go in and out at the same times every day. This can be a real challenge for those of us who don't live routine lives or who find following a schedule more challenging.

But even if your life isn't exactly regimented, you can structure your dog's life according to a schedule. If need be, set a timer or the alarm on your PDA, but let your dog out, feed her, and train her at approximately the same time every day. Even if you don't go to bed at a regular time, put your dog to bed at a regular time. You may find she

Dogs thrive with a regular schedule of eating, sleeping, and outside time.

does this for you. My dog Sally always retires at 7 pm every night, whether I'm in bed with her or not (and I'm invariably not).

Sometimes, dogs can help their humans regulate their schedules, reminding us with pleading eyes or little whimpers or fancy circular jumps in the air, "Hey you! It's 15 minutes past dinner!" Instead of punishing your dog for this kind of behavior and confusing her, feed her on time. Don't let her get to the point where she has to remind you.

Establishing a routine is even more important for an adopted dog who has had her life disrupted and who is probably in dire need of regularity. Change means stress for dogs (some more than others), so "bad" behavior on the part of your new pet could be a cry for help: "Please

Your Adopted Dog's Best Influence

Anticipation

A dog should not be allowed to dominate its owner, which can happen if you feed your dog every time she asks for it. Instead, anticipate mealtimes and feed your dog at the same time every day. Then, if she asks for an early dinner, you can sensibly ignore her pleas to manipulate you. Don't make your dog beg for dinner every night because you forgot to feed her, or she can become confused about the message.

give me a normal life!" Help alleviate your new pet's stress by giving her something she can count on. If you aren't sure how to construct a regular schedule for your dog, here is an example. Please modify this schedule according to your own needs. This one works for my family, but you might prefer something different:

- ✳ 7:00 am: Get up, let dog out
- ✳ 7:30 am: Breakfast for humans
- ✳ 7:45 am: Breakfast for dog
- ✳ 8:00 am: Daily grooming: Brush-down, skin check and ear check, toenail clip if necessary
- ✳ 8:30 am: Humans and dog in car (everyone seatbelted) to take kids to school
- ✳ 9:00 am: Time for work—human at desk, dog under desk
- ✳ 12:00 noon: Lunch break for humans
- ✳ 12:15 pm: 10-minute training session followed by treat for dog
- ✳ 12:30 pm: Let dog out for outdoor playtime or sunning session
- ✳ 2:00 pm: Go out to get mail, dog comes along to check out the front yard
- ✳ 3:30 pm: Kids come home from school, dog playtime
- ✳ 4:00 pm: Yard work and/or house clean-up, dog and kids "helping"

Your Outta Control Adopted Dog

A routine can help your adopted dog feel secure and comfortable in his new home.

* 5:00 pm: 15-minute training session followed by 5-minute play session for dog
* 6:00 pm: Dinner for humans
* 6:30 pm: Dinner for dog
* 6:45 pm: Let dog out
* 7:00 pm: Dog goes to bed
* 8:00 pm: Kids go to bed
* 11:00 pm: Human snuggles with dog, then goes to bed

Even if you sometimes deviate here and there, a regular set-up like the one above will help any adopted dog to feel secure, comfortable, and safe. She will know what is coming, what to expect, and will be happy to remind you when you forget that it is training time, treat time, or time to go out. She will adore you for giving her a schedule and for saving her from her irregular and possibly traumatic past life.

Your Adopted Dog's Best Influence

Routines: For Better or Worse?

People often ask if a regular routine will make a dog more upset when the routine is necessarily disturbed, such as in the case of a family emergency, a special event, visitors, an unexpected trip, a day away from home, a vacation, or anything else that comes up. However, the security a dog learns from a regular routine should make her more adaptable to change, and the occasional change in routine followed by an uneventful return to the routine (not marked by excessive emotion on your part) will teach your dog that, although sometimes things are different, they always go back to the way they were again, and it's nothing to worry about.

When you follow a regular schedule, you can begin to eliminate any behavior problems and start training.

In fact, many behavior problems in adopted dogs are due, at least in part, to the absence of a routine in their lives. Simply establishing one and sticking to it can help resolve all kinds of misbehaviors and other unpleasant conditions like separation anxiety, housetraining accidents, fearful behavior, and hyperactivity.

While your dog may have personality traits you find hard to deal with, living with a routine will at least help to eliminate behavioral problems

Your Outta Control Adopted Dog

that compound with the difficulties of breed-specific traits and lack of training. When your dog can relax and feel secure, you can uncover who she really is and what you really have to work with. You may find your dog isn't nearly as "outta control" as you thought!

The Importance of Training

I cannot emphasize enough the importance of obedience training for an adopted dog. It doesn't matter if your dog's puppyhood is a distant memory. All dogs benefit from regular training, and by regular, I mean every single day. Sure, you can eliminate all kinds of problems by training a puppy from the first day you bring him home, but in the case of your adopted dog, you cannot control what kind of training your dog did or didn't receive in the past.

You cannot control your dog's past, but you can start training your dog and working toward a bright future together.

And, while you can train your dog every day from a book or videotape, nothing beats the hands-on experience of taking your dog to an obedience instructor, whether in private sessions or in a class. An obedience instructor can address your individual situation, your personality, your dog's personality, your dog's breed or mix of breeds, and your living situation. Unlike a book or video, an instructor can watch you as you work, pointing out where you could be doing something differently or better, and can help you to determine how well your dog is responding.

Taking an obedience class also gives you a basic structure for your at-home training sessions. You have things to practice, like homework assignments, and you can try different techniques for behavior modification, as well as basic commands and tricks.

Once again, just because your dog isn't a puppy is no reason not to enroll him in basic obedience. Today is a new day, and it's never too late. It might be more difficult to train your older dog than it would be to train an eight-week-old puppy, but then again, your dog may already have some training knowledge floating around in that canine noggin' and you might not have to start from square one.

A dog who takes an obedience class and who trains with you every single day gets many different benefits from that training, including:

Your Outta Control Adopted Dog

* The chance to bond with you every day;
* The chance to learn how to communicate with you every day;
* The chance to continue socialization by being around other people and dogs in class;
* One more regular element to his comfortable routine;
* Information, gleaned from training, about what you like and what you don't like;
* A job, as well as a sense of importance and usefulness;
* Mental stimulation;
* Physical exercise;
* New skills;
* Better behavior, which results in better dog-human interactions.

Basic obedience and advanced training will give your dog confidence and benefit your relationship.

A Kinder, Gentler Method

Most dogs do better with gentle training methods that include lots of rewards and positive reinforcement, but some dogs that are particularly active, dominant, and strong can benefit from a more structured, rigorous, and discipline-based method. However, avoid any trainer who hits dogs, yanks them around, or does anything else that looks abusive to you. Always feel free to walk out of a class if it takes an uncomfortable turn. Don't pay someone to abuse your dog! Be your dog's advocate and find a trainer that can help you communicate with each other.

If those aren't reason enough to train your dog, consider this: According to the National Council of Pet Population Study and Policy, 96 percent of the dogs surrendered to animal shelters had no formal obedience training. It's easy to extrapolate that if all pet dogs were taken to obedience classes and if all pet owners engaged in daily obedience training sessions for their pets, hardly any would relinquish their dogs. Most animal shelters do all they can to screen potential pet owners carefully, but they can't force you to train your pet. You, however, can dramatically reduce the chances that your pet won't work out in your home if you register your dog in obedience class. It's that simple, and it's that fun!

Most cities have many obedience instructors to choose from, so look for someone who teaches with a method that makes sense to you and doesn't make you uncomfortable. Sit in on a class or two and observe before registering and get recommendations from people who have taken the class. Ask the instructor what credentials and training he or she has. For evidence of a positive trainer, look for members of the

Your Outta Control Adopted Dog

Association of Pet Dog Trainers (APDT), clicker trainers, and those who advocate reward-based training. To find a APDT trainer in your area, call 1-800-PET-DOGS.

Also look for a trainer who isn't so devoted to a particular method that he or she isn't willing to work with you and your dog to find a way that works. Not every method works for every dog-human team.

Last of all, don't forget the part about daily practice. Going to obedience class once a week for eight weeks isn't enough for any dog. Daily practice, during which you and your dog work things out, spend time together, play together, and practice different commands, tricks, and behaviors, is the cement that holds your relationship together. Daily practice reminds your dog how to behave and reminds you to stay in touch with and pay attention to your dog. It builds great habits for both of you and

Advancing in the Ranks

Think basic obedience is enough? Maybe, if you practice every day at home and expand your dog's repertoire of commands and tricks on your own using books, videos, and your own imagination, but why not get inspired by specializing? Advanced obedience, not to mention classes in dog sports like agility and flyball, can be great fun for the two of you and a great way to meet other dog owners and their pets. Or, consider a class to help your dog earn his Canine Good Citizen® certificate through the American Kennel Club (ask your local obedience club about CGC® classes), or to get certified to do pet therapy in hospitals and nursing homes. The world is filled with opportunities for dogs and humans to work together, so why not sample some of the options? Your training will never get boring.

Obedience training can go a long way to helping your dog adjust to his new life and help him feel like a contributing family member.

encourages an almost intuitive communication the longer you do it. Beyond providing your dog with food, water, and basic care, spending 10 or 15 minutes once or twice each day in a lighthearted and fun training session is the most valuable thing you can do to enhance your relationship with your dog and create a bond that will last a lifetime.

Your Outta Control Adopted Dog

How to Socialize Your Adopted Dog

What's the single most important thing you can do for your adopted dog beyond fulfilling his basic needs for food, water, and shelter? What is even more important than obedience training, pampering your pet, giving him cool toys, providing a luxurious dog bed, or feeding gourmet pet treats? What will be most likely to keep him from going back to the animal shelter, being euthanized, being abused, or being the cause of legal action against you? One word: Socialization.

Canine Socialization 101

Socialization is the process of getting a dog used to life among humans, other dogs, and other pets... in other words, life in the world as we know it. Domesticated dogs in the 21st century simply can't act according to their natural doggy instincts as they would in the wild or in a pack where they never encountered humans. Sure, some of those natural doggy instincts are fine, like the ability to follow a scent, play, or bond with their pack members, but some of them must, out of necessity, be modified. Dogs can't play with humans the way they play with other dogs; human skin is too sensitive. They can't challenge us the way they might challenge a pack leader; we aren't up to snarling dominance fights. They can outrun us; but they need to know that when we say, "Come back," they need to obey. They can't go off hunting whatever they see that looks like prey; it might be the family cat. And they certainly can't be afraid of us; otherwise, at worst, they might attack us. At best, they might be so afraid of us that they live lives full of fear and stress.

Socialization begins with the puppy's mother and littermates. Proper socialization from the start will help your puppy get along with other dogs later in life.

Your Outta Control Adopted Dog

How Puppies Learn

Studies conducted back in the 1960s showed that a puppy that was isolated from its mother and littermates from birth (though its needs for food, water and shelter were met) was later unable to recognize other dogs or humans as anything familiar and was unable to get along in any sort of society, dog or human. Puppies learn from their mothers, from their littermates, and from the humans in their lives how to interact. Socialization begins in the whelping box.

The good news is that dogs are smart, thinking creatures that socialize beautifully. Actually, dogs are naturally socialized to pack life in the wild. The trick is to socialize them to life in human society, something dogs enjoy immensely. They love to bond with us, follow our rules, be loyal to us, give and receive affection from us, learn from us, work for

Puppies make associations from their early life that carry throughout their adulthood.

How to Socialize Your Adopted Dog

us, and generally live productively and happily among us. Socialization makes this possible, physically and psychologically, for dogs. Without it, dogs won't and can't thrive among humans, and the result can be disastrous for everyone.

From mother, littermates, and early human interaction, puppies quickly learn what is and isn't appropriate, who should be feared and who can be trusted, which situations are fun and interesting and which are frightening and to be avoided. They learn how to play, make friends, form relationships, and follow rules. Also, if necessary, they learn how to run away, defend themselves, and take over the helm if nobody is leading the pack. Puppies make associations from their early life experience that can last throughout their lives. It's easy to socialize a puppy, but it's tough to repair the damage when a puppy hasn't been socialized or hasn't been socialized enough.

Socialization and Your Adopted Dog

Because a puppy's early experiences are imprinted on her for life, an adopted dog's socialization can be a tricky business. The first eight weeks are extremely important for healthy development later in life. Staying with the mother and littermates long enough to learn how to interact and play with other dogs is essential. The mother teaches her puppies how to follow certain rules and provides the health benefit of nursing until the pups are ready to be weaned. Littermates help each other learn how to play and explore, and they help to map out a sort of primitive puppy social hierarchy. Ideally, while puppies are still in the whelping box, they should also have plenty of frequent, happy contact with humans.

According to animal behaviorist Ian Dunbar, DVM, the author of many books on training and socialization, the first month of a puppy's life is

In order to become socialized, puppies should meet as many different people and animals as possible in the first few weeks of life.

critical for socialization. He recommends that in the first four weeks of life, puppies should meet 100 different people in all shapes, sizes, ages, colors, and gender, including children, people with canes or in wheelchairs, people with beards, people in uniforms, etc. These interactions should all be positive, rewarding, and fun. A puppy with this kind of vast socialization experience coupled with training will grow up to be a well-mannered, confident, friendly dog.

If you buy a puppy from a good breeder who works with the puppies to socialize them to humans before they are ready to leave the mother and littermates, you have a good chance that your puppy will be well socialized. In a perfect world, you would then take this puppy home at about 10 weeks of age and continue to socialize him every single day.

But what about your shelter dog, rescued dog, or stray dog? You've not only missed the first month of her life, you may have missed as much as the first few years. That critical socialization period is completely out

How to Socialize Your Adopted Dog

Tricky Pups

According to the American Pet Association (www.apapets.com), more than half of America's dogs can perform at least one trick.

of your hands. Is that the reason your shelter dog is so hyper, shy, grouchy, or suspicious of strangers?

Maybe—and maybe not. The good news is that while you don't know if your dog received proper socialization, you don't know if she didn't receive it, either. Many dogs in animal shelters were raised by a breeder who socialized them as puppies, but then were sold to people who couldn't handle them as adolescents. Many dogs in animal shelters were long-term, well-behaved family pets. And even those who were strays may have had all kinds of social contact in their colorful past.

Perhaps your pup was found by a child who played with him and loved him. Perhaps as he wandered, his interactions with humans were positive. Even if he had negative experiences with humans, these could have happened late enough in your dog's life (such as after the first six months) that they didn't permanently color your dog's interactions or only affected your dog in certain ways. Maybe your stray dog is happy and friendly but suddenly gets fearful around women, little boys, or large dogs. This is a problem to take very seriously, but you may be able to work through it.

Animal behaviorist and trainer Karyn Garvin once told me that among the best and most well-socialized dogs she sees are those who sit with their masters on the traffic islands next to "Will Work for Food" signs. Karyn tells me, "These dogs are so worldly and street-wise, and have

Your Outta Control Adopted Dog

Whatever your dog's past socialization, you can help him overcome his fears and become a part of the family.

encountered so many different people and situations in their lives that they can handle just about anything. They sit placidly on the traffic island. They aren't hyper. They don't jump on people. They don't run into traffic. They'll even wait there, perfectly well behaved, while their owners go to get a soda. Now that's a well-socialized dog."

So there is hope for your adopted dog, whether she has a checkered past or was a cherished former family pet. In fact, as Karyn Garvin suggests, the dogs with checkered pasts may have a head start on socialization as compared to the pampered little dog who never saw the outside of the house, rarely met anyone new, thinks he is human, won't associate with other dogs, and snaps and bites anyone who even approaches the one person he has bonded to.

Whatever your dog's individual situation, you can begin to repair past socialization snafus and help your dog grow into a more confident, friendly, and safe pet by putting effort into socialization. That effort can be as simple as taking your dog on a daily walk, something you probably do already. The great thing about socialization is that it's fun to do.

Assessing Your Adopted Dog's Social Relationships: A Quiz

Take a look at that adopted dog sitting there at your feet. He's a good dog…except when it comes to (you fill in the blank). For now, don't worry about everyday behavior problems like house soiling or chewing, let's just look at social relationships. Do you have an outgoing dog? A hyper dog? A shy dog? Take this quiz to help you more carefully define what kind of social challenges your dog has and how he responds to relationships in general. For each question, choose the answer that most closely describes your dog.

1. When you first met your adopted dog, how did he/she respond to you?

A. My dog was very shy and submissive. It took a long time to get her to look at me or come to me.

B. My dog was very forward and ran right up to me. She sniffed me, but wouldn't respond to my attempts to get her to sit.

C. My dog was so excited, she wouldn't stop wiggling, jumping, and bouncing around. I couldn't get her to calm down.

D. My dog was very friendly but seemed easily startled by loud noises or sudden movements.

E. My dog was interested in me but very cautious. She watched me very carefully, following my every move, but took awhile to actually let me pet her.

F. My dog kept bowing her head and wouldn't look me in the eye. When I tried to pet her, she immediately rolled over and urinated.

2. Now that your adopted dog has settled into your household, how does he respond to family members?

A. He is particularly bonded to one person. He likes other family members, but they seem to make him a little nervous.

B. He is very confident and likes everyone, but tends to get snappy if somebody approaches him while he is eating or if someone tries to make him get down off the couch or bed.

C. He seems to like family members but doesn't pay all that much attention to anyone. He is always running and bounding around the house or yard.

D. He seems happy but still gets easily startled. He is afraid of certain sounds or objects, such as the vacuum cleaner or thunder, and when something startles him, he disappears. It doesn't matter who tries to coax him out, he won't budge until he's ready.

E. He is happy and friendly around the immediate family but if anybody else comes over, he disappears, backs away, or won't stop barking, even if it is someone he has met before.

F. He rolls over on his back for everyone, lets anyone pick him up, is very obedient, and rarely looks anyone in the eye. Although he is house-trained, he urinates if anybody yells, even if it isn't at him.

The way your dog reacts to certain circumstances and people can tell you a lot about his personality.

3. In general, how does your dog respond to children?

A. She wags her tail a little when she sees children, but stays back from them as if she is nervous or afraid of them.

B. She certainly isn't afraid of them but can get nippy with them, and sometimes pushes them over. Once she even chased a little boy on his bike.

C. She gets extremely excited when she sees children, but is so eager to play with them that she jumps on them, sometimes knocking them over or nipping their clothes or fingers. It seems to be in the spirit of play, but it is overwhelming to the children.

D. She likes children but seems particularly wary of certain kinds of children—teenage boys or wobbly toddlers, for example. Or, she enjoys quiet children but suddenly runs away when children start running around, get very active, or talk loudly.

Your dog should be socialized to children, but always supervise their play together.

Your Outta Control Adopted Dog

E. She seems very suspicious of children, standing out of the way or getting a little growly if they come near. She stays back from them.

F. She always rolls over or gets down low and wags her tail around children, but they seem to really wear her out. When they get too rough, she might run away or roll over and urinate, but she never growls or nips.

4. When company comes to your home, how does your adopted dog act?

A. He hides.

B. He barks and tries to keep them from coming in.

C. He is so hyper and wild that we have to put him away.

D. He's fine with most people, but certain people scare him.

E. He is very reserved and acts suspicious of people until he's seen them many times. Sometimes he growls if someone tries to pet him.

F. He rolls over on his back or cowers.

5. The one thing you most worry about for your adopted dog's future is that:

A. She will always be afraid of people, a shy shivery dog or even a fear biter if she feels cornered.

B. She might someday bite or attack somebody because she is so dominant.

If you have a shy dog, you can help him to adjust by allowing him to meet new people in a gentle, positive, and calming manner.

How to Socialize Your Adopted Dog

C. She will never settle down, and I'll never get to enjoy and relax in her company.

D. She will remain debilitated by her fears.

E. I won't be able to trust her around strangers.

F. She will never be self-confident enough to enjoy new experiences.

Now count up your answers. Just doing this quiz has probably given you an idea of what kind of dog you've got, but let's look at these six socialization profiles in a little more detail.

The Shy Dog

If you circled mostly As, you have a shy dog. Shyness can be a natural part of a dog's temperament, but shy dogs that have lost their homes

often have their natural shyness exacerbated. A dog that wasn't well socialized as a puppy will often be shy, and a dog that was happy and well adjusted can become shy if she suffers some trauma, like abuse or neglect. Shyness is a heartbreaking condition to witness in a dog, because the fear and stress the shy dog is experiencing is obvious. But what do you do about it?

A shy dog that meets happy humans every day and is rewarded for her good behavior will eventually be able to succeed in new situations.

Shy dogs are cautious, defensive, and fearful. They try to avoid new situations and new people, but for this type of dog,

Your Outta Control Adopted Dog

Stay. No. Really - Stay!

According to dog trainer Deborah Wood, author of *Help for Your Shy Dog*, the stay command is one of the most challenging obedience commands for shy dogs because it means you—the one person the shy dog has bonded to and trusts—is walking away. Yet, learning to "stay" is crucial for building your shy dog's confidence, so keep practicing. Increase the distance you walk away in small increments and be patient.

socialization is absolutely crucial. Pampering and cod-dling her will just reinforce the shyness, but happy, positive, gentle exposure every day to those things your shy dog finds frightening will help de-sensitize her. It will help her grow in confidence and courage. Don't force your shy dog to face her fears in an insensitive way, but help her face her fears nevertheless. A shy dog who fears humans will eventually conquer that fear if she meets humans of different types every day of her life, and if that interaction is always positive and rewarding.

The Dominant Dog

If you circled mostly Bs, you have a dominant dog. These dogs can be a real challenge, especially if they are already full-grown, large, and strong when you adopt them. Dominant dogs may have been socialized in a way that taught them that they could control humans, or perhaps the original owner was a passive, unassertive person who wasn't able to handle the dog. However, diligent socialization coupled with consistent training will help your dog learn that he is not the ruler of the house and property.

Dominant dogs become most dangerous when they have not learned bite inhibition. A dominant dog running in a pack of dogs can be even more dangerous, as dogs in a pack can have a heightened prey drive.

How to Socialize Your Adopted Dog

Needless to say, you should never let your dog run loose unsupervised and off-leash. However, you should socialize your dominant dog by taking him into many different situations among different people and other dogs every single day, under controlled conditions. He will learn that you are watching him, supervising him, making the rules, and enforcing them. If you have trouble handling your dominant dog, please seek help from a professional trainer, or if your dog is behaving aggressively, from a trained canine behaviorist specializing in dominance issues. Once your dominant dog learns that you are in charge, he can relax and take life a little easier. You'll have a safer and friendlier pet.

The Hyperactive Dog

If you circled mostly Cs, you have a hyperactive dog. Some dogs that

Some breeds or mix of breeds are naturally more energetic than others.

are naturally energetic and friendly become hyper when they haven't been properly socialized and/or have been starved for attention. This is a common problem with adopted dogs who are young and happy and still in puppyhood (mentally, at least), but haven't been getting enough human interaction. They are so desperate to get it that they lose control, jumping and barking in a frenzy of joy and excitement that someone is actually not-icing them. If they have never been trained not to behave that way, so much the worse.

Your Outta Control Adopted Dog

Hyperactive dogs are tough to socialize because their behavior makes typical socialization activities—walking on a leash, going to the dog park, having people over—difficult and unpleasant. Who wants to be yanked down the street by a hyperactive 70-pound Labrador Retriever or spend a whole dinner party pulling a Brittany down because she won't stop jumping on the guests? Yet, socialization experiences, along with a whole lot of exercise, are exactly what a hyperactive dog needs. If you can meet your hyperactive dog's physical and mental needs, then socialization will become easier.

Lots of socialization combined with lots of exercise will help your hyperactive dog handle the world around him.

Couple daily social ventures with consistent daily training and your hyperactive dog will soon learn that even though she wants to jump, run,

Clinically Hyperactive?

Some dogs actually do have a behavioral disorder in which they are uncontrollably hyperactive and unable to stop moving until they collapse. However, this condition is rare. In most cases, your dog is just exuberant and probably needs more attention, structure, and exercise.

How to Socialize Your Adopted Dog

bark, spin, and race, sometimes it simply isn't appropriate. Also, remember that many dogs calm down significantly by two or three years of age. If your one-year-old adopted dog is hyper, do everything you can to teach her good habits and introduce her to many different people and experiences before she reaches the age of two. Simply having the opportunity to experience daily socialization can be enough to calm down the most hyperactive dogs. All they want is to be involved in your life.

The Fearful Dog

If you circled mostly Ds, you have a dog with specific fears. Some dogs are perfectly confident until that one horrible, menacing nemesis appears, whether it's a thunderstorm, broom, or bicycle. A dog with a specific fear or fears probably associates them with a past experience. Perhaps he was chased with a broom, hit by a bicycle, or lost out in a thunderstorm. As an adopted dog owner, you may never know the source of his specific fear, but, just as with a shy dog, the gentle, gradual, highly

You may never know the original cause of your dog's fears, but you can help him to cope with gentle desensitization.

Your Outta Control Adopted Dog

rewarding exposure to that source of fear is extremely important to help desensitize your dog to what scares him. For example, whenever it begins to thunder, don't coddle and pour sympathy over your dog. Get happy; play; give him some treats; most of all, act like a thunderstorm is the best time you've had all week.

If it's the broom, let your dog sniff the broom. Hide treats in the broom. Smear peanut butter on the broom. Make the broom a strange and wonderful source of yummy things. If it's bicycles, let him hang out with one. Let him sniff it. Stick a chew treat in the spokes. Move it back and forth just a bit. Take your dog on a walk, while walking your bike. You get the picture. These are all socialization strategies that will help socialize your dog to the source of fear, because socialization isn't just about interacting with humans. It's about living successfully in society.

Stop and Drink the Flowers

Flower essences are safe, homeopathic remedies said to contain the essence or energy of different flowers. One remedy made by Bach called Rescue Remedy is specifically formulated to help calm stressed, fearful dogs. If you are interested in natural remedies and holistic health, you might try Rescue Remedy for your fearful dog. Put a few drops in your dog's water every day.

The Suspicious Dog

If you circled mostly Es, you have a suspicious dog. Some breeds are described as "reserved," and this is fine. A dog with a reserved temperament doesn't rush up to greet just anyone. He waits and sees or waits for the OK from you before he accepts somebody into the home. A suspicious dog carries this "reserve" too far. Suspicious dogs don't trust people, and your adopted dog may be suspicious for good reason. Perhaps people have proven themselves unworthy of his trust in the past. That

Your dog will look to you for the guidance and discipline he needs. It is up to you, as his owner, to provide him with a stable and confident role model.

means you have a special challenge: It's now your job to teach your dog that some people—and in fact, many people—can be trusted. While your dog will probably never turn into the type of dog that is so friendly that he wags his tails and runs up to any stranger to say hello, you can teach him that you will keep him safe from harm and that now, in this new phase of his life, people are okay.

A reserved dog can be a valuable watchdog, because they often have a good sense of who is "right" and who is "wrong." However, there is a fine line between the reserved dog, who waits to see if that person coming up the driveway is friend or foe, and the suspicious dog, who just assumes "Foe!" at the approach of any stranger. Suspicious dogs can become biters if they aren't given a stable and secure life and lots of constant positive social interaction in a safe environment. Socialization is crucial for your dog, not only for his own well-being and for the protection of others, but also for you, who could be slapped with lawsuit if your suspicious dog chomps on the UPS guy.

A final note on suspicious dogs: Sometimes they have had past experiences that have so colored their attitudes that they can benefit immensely from the services of a trained animal behaviorist. If you aren't comfortable about handling your suspicious dog on your own, I strongly suggest hiring outside professional help before your he turns into a biter.

Dog Bites and Your Liability

According to attorney Kenneth Phillips, who represents dog bite victims all over the United States (www.dogbitelaw.com/), the laws differ in many places, and for the most part, dog owners are liable for dog bites, even if they follow all laws. Ownership alone is cause for liability. However, there are exceptions in which a dog owner may not be held liable:

* If the bite victim was a trespasser and/or was committing a felony;
* If the victim was a veterinarian treating the dog when bitten;
* If the victim was provoking the dog;
* If the dog was assisting police or military when the bite occurred.

Check your state and local laws to learn about dog bite liability in your area.

The Submissive Dog

If you circled mostly Fs, you have a submissive dog. Many submissive dogs are also shy, and their submissive behaviors are part of that shyness. However, some submissive dogs aren't necessarily shy. They may be happy and even friendly. They just want to make darned sure you know that they are not arguing with you when you tell them you make the rules.

Submissive dogs are actually easy to train because they are so motivated to obey you. However, they also have certain behaviors, like constant cowering and submissive urination, that are inconvenient and annoying to humans. Submissive dogs are right to detect that you are in charge, but they also need to gain enough confidence to get along in the world without being glued to your side. A submissive dog desperately wants to please you, but when you say, "Sit," she may find it impossible to do anything but "roll over." A harsh word or a raised voice can crush her.

Submissive dogs need socialization desperately, so that they can understand that the world is filled with kind, fun humans. Build your submissive dog's confidence by letting her interact with different people and dogs every day rather than keeping her inside where she will feel safe. Just as with shy dogs, submissive dogs don't need to feel safe; they need to feel confident. They need to have experiences that teach them, and they need to have training that helps them succeed.

Hanging out and interacting with your dogs should be part of your everyday routine, and can be very enjoyable for all.

Part of the Family

Now that you understand a little more about your dog's individual needs for social-ization, let's look at some of the best ways to socialize your adopted dog. Remember, you should do something to social-ize your dog every single day for the rest of his life. Socialization should be a daily part of your dog's existence, just like getting his dog food.

When you first bring home an adopted dog, especially one who is causing you some problems, you need to establish a bond of

Your Outta Control Adopted Dog

Your adopted dog should have a place inside your home to call his own, and he should be allowed to live as part of the family.

trust before you start pulling him down the street to meet the neighbors. Whether your dog is shy, submissive, or dominant, socialization to other humans will be most successful if you first socialize your dog to your own family.

Adopted dogs who live inside the house with you will be much better socialized than dogs who live outside in the yard, in a dog house, or in a kennel. Most dogs love to go outside, but if you really want a well-adjusted dog you can trust, you need to let your dog live inside most of the time, like you do. Let him go out for exercise, playtime, a little sun, and a nice walk, but for best results, let your dog spend time with you in the house.

Also, your dog should get to spend individual time with each family member (remember that time with children should always be supervised). Let each family member feed your dog, fill the water bowl,

Sleeping Quarters

Where does your adopted dog sleep? Your dog will probably be most comfortable sleeping in someone's bedroom, and if you don't mind making room, she will probably be happy to join you on the bed. Dominant dogs should be made to sleep on the floor, but can still sleep near you. Shy, submissive dogs may also benefit from a comfortable spot near (but not in) your bed to help increase a sense of independence. A few dogs prefer to sleep outside (although I personally don't think all that many really prefer it). If yours does, be sure to bring him in if he barks at night, and spend plenty of quality time together training and socializing during waking hours so he learns to trust and interact with humans.

give treats, practice training commands, play ball, and come along on walks. Let your dog be constantly surprised by which family member just might have a yummy treat hidden in a pocket—but instruct everyone never to give the dog the treat until he does something for it first, such as sit, lie down, or perform some trick you have taught him. (We ask Sally to "dance," which she does by jumping and doing a 360-degree turn in the air.)

All Shapes and Sizes

Even though it is important to socialize your dog to your own family, don't wait too long before taking him out into the world. Whether your dog is friendly or reserved, he should start meeting new people right away.

Begin socializing your dog to other people in the comfort of your own home. Especially if your adopted dog is still a puppy and hasn't had all

Your Outta Control Adopted Dog

Party On!

One fun way to begin socializing your adopted dog is to have a party. Depending on your dog's personality, your party can be big or small, but have guests come over to meet your new family member, pet him gently, and give him treats. Make it fun and rewarding for your dog to solicit the attention of others, but don't let him get away with chewing on fingers or jumping up on people. Have him sit nicely for petting and instruct guests to ignore him when and if he jumps up. Soon he will learn that sitting nicely and wagging his tail gets him lots of love, affection, and yummy things. And don't forget to provide some yummy human treats for your guests, too, as thanks for helping you out in your socialization efforts.

his vaccinations yet, you don't want to expose him to infectious diseases. Dangerous diseases like parvovirus are most common in areas where other dogs have soiled, so keep young puppies away from the dog park until they are fully vaccinated. However, having people over to your house is an easy way to introduce your adopted dog to human society.

Beyond meeting people, what does socialization actually entail? It's simple: experience. Your dog needs to gain expe-

The more places you take your dog, the better socialized he will become.

rience of many people, situations, and other dogs. Here are some ideas for how to put socialization into practice:

* Walk your dog every day. Stop and talk to neighbors and other pet owners. When you stop, let the dogs sniff each other but supervise in case snarls erupt. When talking to another person who isn't accompanied by a dog, have your dog sit and wait for you to finish talking. Encourage other people to talk to and gently pet your dog before moving on.

* Don't take the same route every time on your daily walks. Go the opposite way around the block, walk through a different neighborhood, drive to a park, or visit other interesting, dog-friendly areas. Keep changing the scenery.

* Don't just walk your dog—walk and train. Stop every block or so and execute a command like sit or lie down, or have your dog perform a trick. Encourage passersby to watch, comment, praise, and even offer treats (carry them in your pocket at all times!).

Your dog should be introduced to gentle children as soon as possible.

* Are there kids in the neighborhood? That's great, especially if you don't have kids at home. Dogs must be socialized to children to ensure against biting, as children are among the most frequent victims of dog bites. However, don't let kids overwhelm your dog, especially if she is shy, but let them come by, one or two at a time, for gentle petting and treats, and always supervise.

Your Outta Control Adopted Dog

* If you walk your child to or from school every day, take your dog along. He'll get to meet lots of different kids. Well-socialized dogs won't be scared or challenged by the chaos of kids in a schoolyard. Always keep your dog on a leash and supervise any child-dog interactions. (Note: Don't take your dog to the schoolyard if he gets nippy with kids. Socialize him to children in a less chaotic, more controlled environment first.)

* Who says you always have to walk your dog? Maybe an older, responsible neighborhood child would like to do it for a few dollars. What about other family members or dog-loving friends? The more people who get to spend time with your dog, the better.

* When you have people over to your house, don't put your dog in his crate or outside unless absolutely necessary. While it may be more convenient, your dog won't learn anything. Instead, keep him on a leash and let him figure out how to act. Don't reward bad behavior, but be sure to reward good behavior.

* Every time you have errands to run, take your dog with you in the car, especially if you can accomplish things using drive-thrus, such as the bank, pharmacy, or fast-food restaurant. (Note: Don't ever leave your dog alone in a parked car in

Take your dog with you—he loves nothing more than being at your side.

How to Socialize Your Adopted Dog

warm weather, as tem-peratures can rise inside your car to dangerous levels in just a few minutes.)

✳ Many pet shops allow dogs. When you go to pick up dog food and supplies, take your dog along and walk him around the store on a leash. Encourage customers to pet him and talk to him. Bring treats!

✳ Many outdoor cafes allow dogs if they sit nicely under your table.

✳ Some cities have dog parks where dogs can go to play together in a fenced area. Pet owners congregate and "talk dog," while the dogs socialize with each other. Dog parks are great for friendly dogs, but can be challenging for shy or dominant dogs. Always supervise interactions and keep your dog on a leash at first until you have a better idea about how he will react. Another option is to visit the dog park during a slow time when you and your dog can play without a big crowd of canines following you around. Dogs who learn to be polite at the dog park are usually quite trustworthy around other dogs.

✳ It's vacation time—how about taking your dog along? Many motels, parks, and even resorts now allow dogs. Just think about the worldly experience your dog will gain from a vacation! Just be sure you keep ID tags and a leash on your dog and carry plenty of food and fresh water.

✳ Does your dog like to swim? Rather than having him encounter water in an insecure situation, introduce him to water as soon as possible. Small lakes and ponds are fun for dogs who might like to fetch a stick or a Frisbee (water retrievers especially enjoy this, but many other dogs do, too). For safety's sake, however, don't try it in a river or ocean where a current could sweep your dog away or when there is ice on the water that could trap your dog. Some dogs even enjoy paddling around a swimming pool, but always supervise them closely and make sure they can get out on their own.

Your Outta Control Adopted Dog

✳ Keep taking your dog to dog-based events like training classes, dog parties, fun matches (dog shows that don't count for points, just for practice), obedience classes, agility classes, dog Halloween parades hosted by the local dog club or humane society, dog washes, and anything else that looks kindly on dogs and their owners.

Have Dog. Will Travel

For more on traveling with your dog, check out www.petswelcome.com, which lists, among other things, hotels, B&Bs, campsites, amusement parks, beaches, festivals, and even bars that are dog-friendly.

Have fun. Make life interesting. After all, why have a dog if you aren't going to really enjoy it?

Swimming is just one of the many activities that dogs love to participate in—find out what your dog likes to do and do it together.

A dog that is socialized to other dogs is a pleasure to take places and will make friends wherever he goes.

Your Adopted Dog and Other Dogs

Companion animal behavior counselor Yody Blass, M.A. advises her clients that puppies should not only meet 100 people but at least 50 other dogs during early socialization. A lack of socialization to other dogs can cause you and your dog many problems, whether you are simply strolling around the block or trying out an afternoon at the local dog park.

Shy dogs can be intimidated by other dogs, especially if they are very small. Help your shy dog conquer her fears by introducing her to kind, gentle dogs, one at a time, but often. Have a friend and her dog over for a "play date." Let the dogs sniff each other, but stay near. When they are ready, let them play. If your shy dog gets very fearful, stay by her but don't let her "win" by taking the other dog away (as long as he is behaving and not being aggressive). Otherwise you will teach her that it is rewarding to be afraid. Continue the contact, gently but relentlessly,

Your Outta Control Adopted Dog

and daily if necessary. Soon your dog will develop a circle of canine friends. The more confidence she gains, the more she will enjoy dog-dog interactions.

Your Adopted Dog and Other Pets

Maybe your adopted dog adores the Lab next door or the Cocker Spaniel down the street but eyes the family cat, your son's hamster, or your sister's spoiled little Chihuahua as if they are furry T-bone steaks. Are your little, furry, suspiciously-resembling-vermin household pets and neighborhood animals safe with your dog?

Doggy Play Group

If you and one or several friends all have dogs, consider organizing a weekly "doggy play group." You can socialize, have coffee or lemonade, and chat while your dogs play together. Always supervise play and be sure all dogs are spayed or neutered and current on their immunizations. If everyone has a fenced yard, rotate locations so the dogs get to play together in different places.

Some breeds were developed over centuries to have an instinct to chase down prey. Whether you've got a leggy, regal Afghan Hound or a tiny little Affenpinscher, many breeds such as these are hunters. Some individuals within a breed may be less interested in laying chase, but other individuals may never be trustworthy around small, quick animals.

However, the flip side of the story is socialization. Many dogs that have a natural prey drive learn to live happily, even affectionately, with the family cat, and in many cases, the family birds. While I would never totally trust a terrier in the room with a ferret or a hamster (there are limits, after all), many dogs can learn to distinguish "random prey" from "family member." If your older adopted dog adjusts easily to your cat, he may well have been raised with a cat. If he acts like he's never seen one before, well...you have your work cut out for you. Again, always supervise and conduct structured contact sessions. In other words, use your good judgment. In some cases, you may just have to keep the two apart.

Your Canine Good Citizen®

One excellent goal for all pet owners working to socialize their adopted dogs is to help their pets earn the Canine Good Citizen® certificate. This certificate and program, developed and implemented by the American Kennel Club (AKC), puts dogs through a series of ten tests to determine how well-behaved, well-socialized and well-trained your dog is. Unlike conformation shows, any dog can take the CGC® test, including dogs adopted from an animal shelter and mixed breeds. A dog who can pass

the ten tests is deemed a Canine Good Citizen® and gets a nice certificate suitable for framing, plus the honor of adding the title "CGC®" after her name, something of which to be very proud.

People trained by the AKC give tests during certain times. You can learn more about the specifics from your local obedience or dog club. Many clubs and trainers also offer classes that train dogs for the CGC® tests. Here is what's required. (The following is

Receiving a Canine Good Citizen® certificate is proof that your adopted dog is a well-trained pet who would be welcomed anywhere.

Your Outta Control Adopted Dog

courtesy of the American Kennel Club.)

Test Item 1: Accepting a Friendly Stranger

This test demonstrates that the dog will allow a friendly stranger to approach him and speak to the handler in a natural, everyday situation. The evaluator walks up to the dog and handler and greets the handler in a friendly manner, ignoring the dog. The evaluator and handler shake hands and exchange pleasantries. The dog must show no sign of resentment or shyness and must not break position or try to go to the evaluator.

Sitting politely for grooming and petting is one aspect of the Canine Good Citizen® test. Getting a CGC® is an admirable goal for any dog and his owner.

Test Item 2: Sitting Politely for Petting

This test demonstrates that the dog will allow a friendly stranger to touch him while he is out with his handler. With the dog sitting at the handler's side, the evaluator pets the dog on the head and body. The handler may talk to his or her dog throughout the exercise. The dog may stand in place as he is petted. The dog must not show shyness or resentment.

Test Item 3: Appearance and Grooming

This practical test demonstrates that the dog will welcome being groomed and examined and will permit someone, such as a veterinarian, groomer or friend of the owner, to do so. It also demonstrates the

How to Socialize Your Adopted Dog

owner's care, concern, and sense of responsibility. The evaluator inspects the dog to determine if he is clean and groomed. The dog must appear to be in healthy condition, i.e., proper weight, cleanliness, general health, and alertness. The handler should supply the comb or brush commonly used on the dog. The evaluator then softly combs or brushes the dog, and in a natural manner, lightly examines the ears and gently picks up each front foot. It is not necessary for the dog to hold a specific position during the examination, and the handler may talk to the dog, praise him, and give encouragement throughout.

Test Item 4: Out for a Walk (Walking on a Loose Lead)

This test demonstrates that the handler is in control of the dog. The dog may be on either side of the handler. The dog's position should leave no

doubt that the dog is attentive to the handler and is responding to the handler's movements and changes of direction. The dog need not be perfectly aligned with the handler and need not sit when the handler stops. The evaluator may use a pre-plotted course or may direct the handler/dog team by issuing instructions or commands. In either case, there should be a right turn, left turn, and an about turn with at least one stop in between and another at the end. The handler may talk to the dog along the way, praise the dog, or give commands in a

Your dog should be able to walk nicely on a leash without pulling and sit calmly while you speak to others.

Your Outta Control Adopted Dog

normal tone of voice. The handler may sit the dog at the halts if desired.

Test Item 5: Walking Through a Crowd

This test demonstrates that the dog can move about politely in pedestrian traffic and is under control in public places. The dog and handler walk around and pass close to several people (at least three). The dog may show some interest in the strangers but should continue to walk with the handler, without evidence of over-exuberance, shyness, or resentment. The handler may talk to the dog and encourage or praise the dog throughout the test. The dog should not jump on people in the crowd or strain on the leash.

Test Item 6: Sit and Down on Command, Staying in Place

This test demonstrates that the dog has training, will respond to the handler's commands to sit and down, and will remain in the place commanded by the handler (sit or down position, whichever the handler prefers). Prior to this test, the dog's leash is replaced with a line 20 feet long. The handler may take a reasonable amount of time and use more than one command to get the dog to sit and then lie down. The evaluator must

FYI on CGC

Check out the CGC® website at: www.akc.org/love/cgc for more detailed information about the test, and to find out where tests may be held near you.

You're Never Too Old

Dogs must be old enough to have been fully vaccinated, including the rabies vaccine, before they may take the CGC® test; however, no dog is ever too old. Even a senior dog can earn his CGC® certificate.

For his safety, your dog should come to you when called.

determine if the dog has responded to the handler's commands. The handler may not force the dog into position but may touch the dog to offer gentle guidance.

When instructed by the evaluator, the handler tells the dog to stay and walks forward the length of the line, turns, and returns to the dog at a natural pace. The dog must remain in the place in which he was left (the dog may change position) until the evaluator instructs the handler to release the dog. The dog may be released from the front or the side.

Test Item 7: Coming When Called

This test demonstrates that the dog will come when called by the handler. The handler will walk 10 feet from the dog, turn to face the dog, and call the dog. The handler may use encouragement to get the dog to come. Handlers may choose to tell the dog to "Stay" or "Wait," or they may simply walk away, giving no instructions to the dog.

Your Outta Control Adopted Dog

Test Item 8: Reaction to Another Dog

This test demonstrates that the dog can behave politely around other dogs. Two handlers and their dogs approach each other from a distance of 20 to 30 feet, stop, shake hands and exchange pleasantries, and continue on for about 10 feet. The dogs should show no more than casual interest in each other. Neither dog should go to the other dog or its handler.

Test Item 9: Reaction to Distraction

This test demonstrates that the dog is confident at all times when faced with common distracting situations. The evaluator will select and present two distractions. Examples of distractions include dropping a chair, rolling a crate dolly past the dog, having a jogger run in front of the dog, or dropping a crutch or cane.

The dog may express natural interest and curiosity and/or may appear slightly startled but should not panic, try to run away, show aggressiveness, or bark. The handler may talk to the dog and encourage or praise him throughout the exercise.

Test Item 10: Supervised Separation

This test demonstrates that a dog can be left with a trusted person, if necessary, and will maintain training and good manners. Evaluators are encouraged to say something like, "Would you like me to watch your dog?" and then take hold of the dog's leash. The owner will go out of sight for three minutes. The dog does not have to stay in position but should not continually bark, whine, or pace unnecessarily, or show anything stronger than mild agitation or nervouness.

Equipment

All tests must be performed on leash. Dogs should wear well-fitting buckle or slip collars made of leather, fabric, or chain. Special training

Your dog should be able to be separated from you without feeling upset or stressed out. Basic obedience can help you work toward a happy and well-behaved pet.

collars such as pinch collars, head halters, etc. are not permitted in the CGC® test. The evaluator supplies a 20-foot lead for the test. The owner/handler should bring written proof of rabies vaccines and the dog's brush or comb to the test.

Encouragement

Owners/handlers may use praise and encouragement throughout the test. The owner may pet the dog between exercises. Food and treats are not permitted during testing, nor is the use of treats, squeaky toys, etc. to get the dog to do something.

Socialization is a lifelong process, so no matter how much or how little your adopted dog has already, continue it every single day. Never forget that socialization is even more important than training. It doesn't matter how much you love your dog, how much your dog loves you, or

What Makes a Dog Fail
the CGC® Test?

If your dog fails to pass any of the ten tests, he fails the entire test, but he may take it again as many times as necessary. In addition, any dog that eliminates during testing will fail, unless he does so during the last test, but only when this test is held outdoors. Finally, according to the AKC, "Any dog that growls, snaps, bites, attacks, or attempts to attack a person or another dog is not a good citizen and must be dismissed from the test."

what anybody's intentions are. If a dog can't live and behave in human society, he won't last long. Let your dog become the canine good citizen you know he can be.

Practical Solutions to Outta Control Problems

It's finally time to get down to the nitty gritty. Your dog is great, but she's got a few problems—the kind of problems that may seem insurmountable and that may have landed your dog in the shelter or rescue group in the first place. Frankly, she may have the kind of problems that cause many people to give up their pets. But you don't want to give up your dog. You want help and you want it now. This is the chapter for you.

This chapter is about training, but not obedience training. This is "house rules" training. Learning how to sit, lie down, and heel are all things you can learn from a basic obedience class, which, as I've said, every adopted dog and her human should attend. These commands are great for dogs to know, and many are crucial for safety. Obedience classes also will also help you deal with behavioral problems and lay a foundation for your "house rules" training. They will also put you in touch with trainers and other dog owners who can further help you.

But lack of obedience training is not the immediate problem. You probably don't think your dog is outta control because she won't sit. You think she's outta control because she pees on the bed, eats your shoes, or jumps over your fence and runs away. Here are some solutions to get you started on a lifetime of good manners and human-friendly behavior.

Your dog may be outta control, but you should never be. Always remain composed when training or disciplining your dog.

Work with your dog every day on her problems and don't give up. Dogs are smart—they can learn if you show them how and make it in their immediate best interest to do so.

Before you start, remember the most important rule: Anger and violence don't work. Sure, you might scare your dog so much that she is afraid to do anything, but rubbing her nose in an accident, swatting her because she ate a pillow, or screaming at her when she comes home after running away can actually have the opposite effect of what you planned. Your dog may be

Your Outta Control Adopted Dog

outta control, but you should never be. You need to control how you behave and communicate with your dog to help her behave in a way that everyone can live with.

Housetraining Horrors

One of the main complaints of people who relinquish their dogs at animal shelters is housetraining problems. Some dogs don't understand where they are supposed to go "potty" because they've never been taught. Even as adults, they may have lived their lives outside and were able to go whenever and wherever they chose. Once they come into your home, they have no idea that you don't like them to use the living room carpet as a bathroom.

Some dogs have been house-trained but relapse due to trauma, medical problems, or fear, or even to test you (this is common in adolescence). Of course, young puppies have yet to learn housetraining and need to be taught, whether they came from an animal shelter or a dog breeder.

However, your dog is still leaving piles in the house or urinating in the kitchen. You can't tolerate that kind of behavior. So what's a committed adopted dog owner to do?

While many adopted dogs were housetrained as puppies, they may lapse in new or stressful situations or because of medical problems.

Medical Reasons for Housetraining Problems

In most cases, house-training problems are easy to fix. However, if your dog urinates far more than seems normal and can't seem to control his bladder, he could have a medical problem. See your vet to rule out a health condition like a urinary tract infection, diabetes, or incontinence (more common in senior dogs).

First, and most importantly, please don't rub your dog's nose in her messes. This makes absolutely no sense to your dog, except perhaps to show her exactly where she went and possibly even re-emphasize to her that she should continue to soil that very spot. Violence like this from you only frightens your dog and causes her to mistrust you. Rubbing her nose or pointing her nose toward the misdemeanor does not send the desired message to your dog.

Fortunately, housetraining is usually a pretty easy problem to fix. The reason so many people have a problem with it is that they simply don't know how to communicate to the dog what is and isn't acceptable. Unless your dog has a medical problem, you can housetrain your dog. I suggest the following two methods—the crate training method and the schedule method. All dogs are different, so one method may work better than another. Also, because all dogs have differently sized bladders and different temperaments, be patient. Some dogs learn quickly, others take awhile. The trick is to stay so vigilant that you never put your dog in a position to make a mistake. If she does have an accident, remember that it is your lapse, not hers.

Crate Training

If you adopted a young, healthy, trauma-free puppy, crate training is by far the most effective method for housetraining. All you need is a dog crate that is big enough for your puppy to stand up, turn around, and lie

Your Outta Control Adopted Dog

Toy Dog Trouble

Toy dogs are notorious for being difficult to housetrain. In many cases, pet owners are probably just more indulgent of toy dog housetraining mishaps because they are so small and easy to clean, and it is easier for a small dog to sneak off and do his business where you can't see him. People also tend to indulge toy dogs in general. However, housetraining a toy dog is no different than housetraining a large dog. It may take a little bit longer, but if you are firm and consistent, and don't let your toy dog make a mistake, he'll get it. Toy dogs may be little, but they are smart and good at figuring out exactly what they can get away with. Teach them that housetraining isn't negotiable.

Many dogs are given up because of housetraining problems; however, with a regular schedule and lots of supervision, any healthy dog can be housetrained.

Practical Solutions to Outta Control Problems

A crate is a valuable housetraining tool because dogs do not like to soil where they eat or sleep.

down comfortably in, but not so big that he can lie in one side and use the other side for a potty. The Nylabone® Fold Away Pet Carrier is very convenient because it can fold up when you're not using it for easy storage.

Most dogs will not soil where they sleep, so the theory behind crate training is that puppies will wait until they are out of their crates to do their business. The trick is to get your puppy to see his crate as a den. Dogs need and seek out sheltered places for protection, and dogs without crates often hunker down under kitchen tables, desks, or chairs. Dogs have a natural instinct to rest in this kind of safe haven, so from the first day you bring your puppy home, associate positive experiences with the crate. Make it comfortable with blankets or a cushion, put a few fun toys inside, and hide a treat in there every so often as a nice surprise.

Until he is housetrained, your puppy should sleep in his crate at night and be in his crate when you cannot supervise him. The crate can sit right next to your bed so your puppy can hear your voice and even see you as you reach down to comfort him. The first few nights your puppy may whine and cry, and you may worry that the crate is becoming associated with negative feelings, but don't be concerned. As long as you remain calm, happy, and reassuring, your puppy will soon grow to love his den.

Your Outta Control Adopted Dog

Crates Aren't Cruel, Unless...

Some people think crates are inherently cruel. I've heard all kinds of comments like, "Well, I would never lock up my dog in one of those things!" What these people don't understand is that dogs love the safety and security of a comfy crate. However, crates can easily become cruel if you use them as an excuse to ignore your dog. No dog will thrive in a crate for ten hours a day, even if he does manage not to soil it. Dogs need attention, human interaction, exercise, and mental challenges. If you work all day and keep your dog in a crate when you are away, come home for lunch or hire a pet sitter or dog walker to come in and let out your dog. Life spent in a crate all day every day is no life for anyone.

Try these steps to crate training your dog:

* When you can't supervise your dog, put him in the crate. Remember that a young puppy can't be expected to go for more than a few hours without needing to relieve himself, so don't stick him in his crate and ignore him for too long.

* Every time you take him out of his crate, immediately take him outside and wait, watching closely, until he relieves himself. Tell him to "go potty" (or whatever words you choose) as he starts to go, then praise him effusively while he's actually doing it: "Go Potty! Whatta good dog!"

* During the day, or whenever your puppy is out of the crate, constantly supervise him. Watch for signs that he needs to go, such as sniffing, circling, and of course, squatting.

* If your puppy looks ready, quickly whisk him outside, otherwise completely ignoring his behavior. As he goes on the grass, say "Go potty! Good dog." If you catch him mid-stream in the house, a quick, sharp "No!" is all you need to say before taking him

Make sure your dog has plenty of time to eliminate outside in order to avoid accidents in the house.

outside. Then, when he finishes, praise him.

✳ Make sure you offer him plenty of opportunities to go outside, taking him out after he eats, drinks, naps, plays, or is in his crate for any period of time.

Remember, if your puppy goes inside the house, it is because he is still learning and you weren't watching the signs. Sure, we all get caught by surprise now and then, which is why constant supervision and quick action are so important. But, as I've said before, dogs are smart. The ones that don't seem smart are probably just independent. They will get it if you do your duty, which is to communicate to them what is okay and what isn't. Dr. Ian Dunbar likes to say that new puppy owners should never allow their pets to have an opportunity to make a mistake. If your puppy does have an accident, he isn't to blame. You are. If you are going to scold somebody, go look in the mirror. Don't take it out on your puppy.

Your Outta Control Adopted Dog

Paper Training

If you plan to have your dog paper trained or litter box trained, you can still use the crate. Do
everything the same, except that the spot to which you
whisk away your dog becomes a specified place in the home
on papers or in the litter box (check your pet store for
these innovative litter boxes made just for small dogs)
instead of outside. It's the same technique and the same
principle.

The Schedule Method

While I find crate training to work wonders with young puppies, crate
training isn't for everyone, nor is it for every dog. Not all adult dogs or
even older puppies require crate training, and some adopted dogs are
highly resistant to the crate. Other dogs who are older may be almost
housetrained, soiling in the house only occasionally. You may feel that

Regular walks can help put your dog on a reliable schedule and
can be good exercise for both you and your pet.

Practical Solutions to Outta Control Problems

Training the Bladder

The older a dog gets, the longer he can hold his bladder, until he hits old age, when the amount of time begins to lessen again. Some adult dogs only need to go out twice a day, which is convenient for those who can't easily go outside or have working owners. However, be patient with puppies and with senior dogs, who aren't physically capable of holding it for more than a few hours at a time.

your adult dog can learn with some consistency but without the crate, which is fine. I didn't have to crate train Sally (although she has a crate, which she finds comforting when the neighbors dog-sit her, and which she loves to nap in on occasion).

For some dogs, a crate is even traumatic. Though they may love to sit in the den-like space under your desk when you work, a crate may frighten these fearful dogs. It's hard to judge which dogs will react negatively to crates, and while it's important to help a dog face her fears, forcing her into a terrifying situation to accomplish housetraining just doesn't make sense. I don't mean to make it sound as if crate training can't work for an adult dog. For some, it is the ideal method. However, adopted dogs are fond of schedules and routines, so you can housetrain your dog by putting him on a schedule.

First, the type of food you feed your dog is very important when putting him on a schedule. You need to feed your adopted dog a good-quality dog food that agrees with his stomach, preferably one that he was accustomed to eating in the shelter or rescue home before he came to live with you. Changing your dog's food suddenly can give him stomach upset and diarrhea, which throws housetraining way off course. Also, be sure to feed him at the same times every day. This can better help you to predict when he needs to eliminate.

If you always let your dog out at the same times every day, he will have no reason to go in the house at any other time. Start out with a schedule that allows your dog more times to relieve himself than he probably needs, just in case. After a few weeks of this schedule (or even a few days, depending on your dog), you'll have a better idea about your dog's individual pattern. Here's a sample schedule for an older puppy, adolescent, or adult dog, for the first few weeks:

* First thing in the morning, let your dog out. Watch him until he goes, then praise.
* Feed him breakfast. About 15-30 minutes after breakfast (you may need to experiment with this number to determine how long after a meal your dog is likely to need to go), let him out again. Watch him until he goes, then praise.

Always feed and water your dog at the same time every day and take him outside to eliminate immediately after.

Practical Solutions to Outta Control Problems

* After you eat lunch, let your dog out. If you are not home or cannot get home during the day, arrange for a neighbor or a dog sitter to take him out. Watch him until he goes, then praise.
* In the afternoon, take your dog on a walk. (Don't forget to bring that plastic baggie!) When he goes, praise him.
* Feed him dinner. About 15-30 minutes after dinner (or as according to your dog), let him out. Watch him until he goes, then praise.
* Right before bed, let him out one last time. As before, watch until he goes, then praise.

This allows your dog six opportunities for "potty breaks" during the day. That should be plenty, unless your dog has a medical problem. Eventually, you may be able to let your dog out only half this many

Your dog should be in his crate when you cannot supervise him. Provide him with toys and Nylabones® to make it a pleasant experience for him.

Your Outta Control Adopted Dog

times, but your job is to observe your dog's habits carefully and craft a schedule that works with this natural process. As long as you give your dog ample opportunity, he won't need to go in the house.

Chewing Woes

You come home after a long day of work, looking forward to seeing your new friend, and lo and behold—the couch has been eaten. Destructive chewing can infuriate humans, but your adopted dog doesn't know that. To him, all alone all day, at best bored, at worst scared and anxious, the couch looked like a way to relieve some tension and fill his time. It worked for him; yet, this kind of behavior obviously isn't acceptable. What can you do about it?

All puppies need to chew to develop mentally and physically.

Practical Solutions to Outta Control Problems

How to Nip Destructive Chewing

Practically all puppies chew. They need to chew to explore the world and relieve teething pain. Many dogs outgrow destructive chewing in the first year, but if your adopted dog is older and still loves to chew and destroy, you may think you've got an insurmountable problem. Adult dogs chew for different reasons, but most often they chew because they are either bored silly and looking for something stimulating to amuse them (which is fixable), or they are missing you, either mildly or frantically, and chewing up something of yours reminds them of you (which is also fixable). There are a few simple solutions to chewing problems.

* Constantly provide your dog with a rotating inventory of interesting, attractive, and chew-worthy toys that he is allowed to chew.
* When you can't supervise your dog, don't allow him access to anything you don't want him to chew.

Most dogs will chew on anything, so only give him access to safe chew toys.

* One of the most important things you can do to keep your dog from chewing while you are gone is to give your dog vigorous exercise before you leave. A tired dog will be napping, not looking for trouble.

First, let's consider the bored dog. When you leave, or even when you are home but aren't giving your dog anything to do, your dog can get bored. Some dogs are happy to sleep the day away, but others—particularly the more active breeds, such as

Doggy Daycare

For help finding a *dog daycare* facility near you, check out the Professional Association of Dog Daycare website at www.daycare4dogs.org/, which lists dog daycare facilities and gives you lots of information about this invaluable service.

German Shepherds, Labrador Retrievers, and Bloodhounds, to name just a few—don't just desire but require something to keep them occupied. You can't just leave your new dog home all day and expect him to behave without setting limits and putting rules in place.

For one thing, no dog should be left alone all day long on a regular basis. If you have to work, come home for lunch. If you can't, consider hiring a pet sitter or even enrolling your dog in one of the many doggy daycare

Good chewing habits will ensure that your dog has healthy teeth throught his lifetime.

centers popping up all over the country. Why should your dog have to just sit there all day long with nothing to do? You can hardly blame him for making his own fun.

What's fun for your dog? Toys—all dogs need toys. Toys aren't just a luxury, they are a necessity for keeping your dog mentally stimulated. Some dogs love their balls, ropes, and stuffed animals, but toys that present a challenge to your dog are the best for keeping him occupied.

When you can't supervise him, put your puppy in a crate with toys to keep him busy and out of trouble.

Toys that you can stuff with food create an interesting challenge for your dog, such as a Nylabone® Rhino stuffed with peanut butter or cheese. He must try to find a way to get all the food out of the toy. That can take some serious thought (and lots of licking!). One toy I like is the Nylabone® Crazy Ball, which dispenses pieces of kibble a little at a time as the dog rolls the ball around the room. Other balls and cubes dispense treats, make funny noises, or roll in strange, irregular ways to surprise your dog.

Location, Location, Location

Now let's look at where you keep your dog when you can't supervise him. Some dogs can be trusted to roam the house freely when you leave, but many can't. It usually takes only one afternoon alone in the house to figure out if your dog can be trusted while you are gone. If you can't

Your Outta Control Adopted Dog

trust your adopted dog, you are in good company. Remember that trusty crate your dog loves to rest in? For the destructive chewer, the crate is a great place to rest while you are away—but only for a few hours at a time, and only after a good morning workout.

Hide and Seek

Dogs love surprises, if they involve treats! Before you leave the house, hide treats around the room in different places for your dog to find.

Some dogs are fine when kept confined to one or two rooms with plenty of toys, comfy spots to nap, and a radio playing. Just make sure that the rooms are dog-proofed, safe, and don't contain anything you care too much about.

Once you have conquered your chewing problem, your dog may be able to roam the house freely, but many never are. Accepting the fact that your dog needs to stay in his crate when you are away can alleviate everybody's stress.

Separation Anxiety

Separation anxiety is a condition in which a dog is so bonded to the owner that any separation is extremely stressful to the dog, often resulting in destruction, housetraining accidents, and the refusal to eat. Dogs can appear extremely panicked or morbidly depressed.

Separation anxiety is basically a fear-based behavior, even if your dog doesn't act afraid. Your dog depends on you for leadership and companionship. When you leave, the dog is (temporarily) without a leader and becomes nervous or frightened. It is the dog's despondency at an unfulfilled expectation: She wants you, and you aren't there. That's frustrating and can provoke anxiety.

Adopted dogs tend to become very bonded to their new owners. Many adopted dog owners believe their dogs seem to know they have been rescued or "saved." While the dog probably doesn't envision his "rescue" the way a human would, adopted dogs are often insecure and particularly needy. They may fear a repeat performance of their abandonment, and when you leave them—it's bound to happen, even if you work at home—they may fear that you won't return.

Separation anxiety is a common problem in adopted dogs, and it can become quite severe. The anxiety in dogs suffering from this problem can be so intense that it can drive them to destroy your possessions; howl, bark, and whine for hours on end; soil the house; or even mutilate themselves through repetitive and obsessive licking, biting, and scratching. Separation anxiety is bad for a dog's health, and it's no good for cultivating friendly neighborhood relations, either. But what can you

Adopted dogs can become very bonded to their people and may suffer anxiety when left alone. Beethoven waits patiently for his owners.

Your Outta Control Adopted Dog

Severe Separation Anxiety

In severe cases of separation anxiety, see your vet about temporary medication options to help calm your dog so that behavioral modification can work. Some of the medications commonly prescribed to dogs to help ease separation anxiety are the same medications prescribed to humans for anxiety or depression, but never give your dog human medication without a specific pre-scription from your vet. Using the wrong medication or administering the wrong dosage could be harmful or even fatal to your pet.

do? You can't take your dog everywhere you go, so sometimes she's got to go it alone for a few hours.

The best way to help your dog to overcome her separation anxiety with a simple basic practice: Tone down your trans-itions! If your leaving becomes a source of high emotion for your dog, your absence will be even more difficult. It's tough to ignore your dog when you leave, especially if you know she will be upset and stressed when you are gone, but try these steps:

To help your dog cope with separation, tone down your transitions and do not become overly emotional when you leave or return to your home.

* If you must, say goodbye to your dog but make it about 15 minutes before you actually leave.

Sally's Separation Saga

When I first moved into a new home, my adopted dog Sally would sit at the pane of glass next to the front door and make squeaky, desperate, coyote-like yelping sounds whenever I left. The whole cul-de-sac could hear, even from inside the house. About 10 minutes before I leave, I now tell her, "Sally has to stay," and she immediately rolls over into a submissive position and wags her tail, indicating she understands. When I leave, I don't even look at her. She trots back to the bedroom and takes a nap until I return.

* When you actually leave, do so matter-of-factly and without looking at or talking to your dog.

* When you return home, ignore your dog for about 15 minutes after coming in the door. Again, matter-of-factly go about your routine, putting away your car keys, hanging up your coat, and checking your messages.

* After you've settled in, sit down and give your dog a friendly but not overly emotional hello.

To humans, not saying goodbye somehow seems rude, but it is not rude behavior to a dog. It's kind behavior, and it shows your dog that you are in control of the situation and that he has nothing to fear. If your dog doesn't associate dramatic emotional experiences with your coming and going, if he doesn't feel and experience your worry and concern, he will be less likely to get himself all worked up and anxious about being alone.

In addition to this all-important practice of ignoring your dog during transitions to and from your home, you can also address certain specific behaviors your dog engages in when you are away.

Secure your dog in his crate or in a safe room when you leave, or if that's not possible, consider taking him with you.

* If you will be gone for only a couple of hours, let your dog rest and relax safe and secure in his crate. A dog won't soil his sleeping quarters or destroy things if he is in his crate.

* For adopted dogs that can't or won't adjust to a crate, secure them in a safe, quiet, and relatively destruction-proof room without a view to the outside, where sights and sounds could trigger barking. The room should contain comfortable things your dog knows, including his crate or bed, fresh water, and some interesting toys he enjoys.

* Consider playing a TV or radio while you are away. The noise could comfort your dog, making him feel like someone is home.

* Putting him in his crate or confining him is equivalent to saying good-bye, so make sure you do so 15 minutes before you leave, and don't make a big deal about it. Rather, make it fun. Perhaps

Practical Solutions to Outta Control Problems

he gets a treat or gets a special toy, like a Rhino® stuffed with peanut butter, but only when he goes in his special place. Soon your pet will learn that your leaving can actually be rewarding, not terrifying.

Clingy Companions

Some dogs are clingy, which can be breed characteristic. An Italian Greyhound will be more likely to follow you around, hovering next to your ankles, than a Jack Russell Terrier, who has plenty of important business to accomplish around the house today, thank you very much. A burly Bulldog is likely to demand your attention as he pins you down (mistaking themselves for lapdogs as they so often do) much more enthusiastically than a Saluki, who will sit regally and watch out the window like a cat, monitoring your movements with the occasional, barely perceptible flick of his placid gaze.

Some adopted dogs can be insecure and cling to you for reassurance. Help your dog build his confidence by leaving him alone with fun things to do.

Of course, there are always exceptions. However, the simple fact is that dogs need your attention. Once you've committed to your adopted dog, you have committed to spending time together. If you've got an emotionally needy dog, so be it. That doesn't mean you are doomed to being physically attached to your dog 24 hours a day. You can help your Velcro dog gain confidence and indep-

Your Outta Control Adopted Dog

endence. He may never be as independent as a cat, but then again, you *did* adopt a *dog.*

Constantly harassing you for attention or pressing against your side can be signs that your dog isn't getting enough attention from you, or that he is afraid he will lose you. Adopted dogs commonly suffer from both these conditions if they didn't get enough attention from a previous owner and then lost that owner. Your adopted dog needs to learn that you will spend enough time with him, and that you aren't going anywhere.

Make sure that you spend enough quality time with your dog so that he gets the attention that he needs.

As with a dog who suffers from separation anxiety, you can gradually de-sensitize your Velcro dog to your constant presence by leaving him alone—in his crate with lots of fun treats and toys or in an enclosed room with fun doggy things to do. At first leave him for very short periods of time, and then gradually increase the duration. When you return, don't make a big fuss over your dog. Ignore him for a few minutes, then greet him and play with him a little, but don't fawn all over him. This can make him feel even more worried and, consequently, even needier.

Otherwise, be sure you are spending enough time with your pet on walks, training, socialization, and play. You adopted a dog for companionship, right? So let him do his job!

Practical Solutions to Outta Control Problems

Some dogs require more mental and physical stimulation than others. Training and exercise are the keys to dealing with your dog's energy level.

Hyperactivity

Remember in the last chapter when we talked about the hyperactive dog? If your dog is the Energizer Bunny (he keeps going and going and going), you may get so worn out that you can't stand the thought of one more game of ball or one more lap around the block. Some dogs have extremely high energy and activity needs. Working, herding, and sporting dogs are among those that sometimes have the compulsion to keep on going until they drop.

Excessive energy is often a function of not getting enough exercise. "But we ran for five miles today!" you may protest. Great (for you and your dog)! A long daily run (or two) should be enough exercise for most dogs, but it may not provide your dog with the additional necessary mental stimulation. That's where training comes in.

Your Outta Control Adopted Dog

Dogs with a whole lot of energy and drive need something to do. They need to work their minds as well as their muscles, and it's up to you to provide them with an outlet for all that energy. If you haven't already, please take your energizer bunny to obedience classes. When you graduate, register for the advanced class. When you graduate, register for agility or specialize in some activity your dog excels in. If your Whippet won't stop racing around the yard, teach him lure coursing. If your Springer Spaniel won't stop chasing birds, try out field trials. If

Energizer Bunny Hall of Fame

While any breed can have energetic individuals, the following breeds are particularly notorious for requiring lots and lots of vigorous activity:

Border Collies
Brittanys
Dalmatians
Golden Retrievers
Irish Setters
Jack Russell Terriers
Labrador Retrievers
Siberian Huskies

Take advantage of your dog's natural energy and train him to participate in sports such as agility.

your Beagle is constantly chasing a scent, try tracking. If your Jack Russell Terrier never stops bouncing up and down, he may be an agility whiz in the making. If your Husky paces, whines, and tries to escape, try sledding or skijoring. Maybe your Pit Bull would really love the mental and physical exertion of weight pulling.

There are so many different dog sports out there that take so much energy and are so much fun that they seem custom-made for energy-rich dogs. Most of them accept any breed of dog, although certain clubs hold events that require dogs to be registered purebreds. Do a little research and invest the time and energy it takes to get involved in canine sports. That hyperactive adopted dog of yours may just be a star athlete in disguise, and you might find a whole new world of friends and fun.

Hairy Houdini, the Escape Dog

The Velcro dog is so happy to be with you that he would never dream of running away. However, his exact opposite is Hairy Houdini, the escape artist extraordinaire. These dogs can jump over or dig under any fence, open doorknobs, even undo latches. Some work in tandem with their buddies and take off together. You may begin to suspect that you know exactly why your adopted dog landed in the animal shelter: He ran away!

Why some dogs have this urge to break free and explore the wide world is a mystery. Some adopted dogs are used to escaping and running away because it has been all they have known. Many dogs probably run away because they are bored and have nothing better to do. If the yard isn't fun, then surely somewhere else will be more stimulating!

Running away can become a real problem in adolescence. Make sure your dog is neutered. In the case of unaltered males, the scent of a female in heat is so powerful that there may be nothing to hold him back. You need to be reasonable about the health and welfare of your adopted dog and have him or her spayed or neutered immediately.

No matter the reason, the fact is that an escaped dog is in danger, and it's your job to protect him. If you have an escape artist living in your home, you must take certain precautions:

Many adopted dogs are used to running away, but the habit can be controlled.

* Have your dog microchipped by a vet or the animal shelter so that even if he is without a collar, he can be identified.

* Make sure your dog is always wearing an ID tag on his collar that lists your phone number.

* Fence your yard. Preferably, have the fence buried at least one foot into the ground or pour a cement foundation around the fence. Make sure the fence is tall enough to prevent jumping. (Some dogs will even foil these efforts. Sally jumps my chainlink fence like it isn't even there.)

* Never walk your runaway dog off-leash. Some dogs get so distracted by their environments that they run off, deaf to your pleas to "Come!" no matter how well trained they are.

* Know your neighbors. If everyone on your block knows about your dog and his wayward wanderlust, you'll have others watching out for him and helping to send him back to you.

* Always think ahead. If your dog scoots out the front door, put him

Practical Solutions to Outta Control Problems

A secure fenced-in yard is a necessity for your adopted dog's safety and well-being.

away before you open it or when you are expecting somebody. If your dog jumps over your fence, go outside with him, watch him while he plays, then bring him back in.

✸ Consider a vibration collar, which vibrates to let your dog know he is getting too close to the boundaries of the yard. These collars come in different types, but the instructions will tell you how to train your dog to stay within the perimeter.

Many dogs run away or display behavior problems because of boredom. If your dog spends long periods of time outside alone, make sure he has plenty of toys to keep him occupied.

If your dog does escape and you have to pick him up at the animal shelter and pay a fee, remember, it was your lapse, not his. Don't blame him. Instead, continue to work with him, train him, and teach him.

Barking Problems

Barking can be a huge problem for a new dog owner, especially an apartment dweller or anyone in a suburban neighborhood where people do not appreciate that sort of noise. However, there is a difference between normal dog barking and excessive dog barking.

First of all, some breeds bark more than others. Terriers are notorious barkers, and you will probably never be able to keep your terrier silent most of the time. It's part of their heritage and part of their character. Many herding breeds also bark because that has always been a crucial part of herding, and they retain that instinct. Any dog will bark when they feel they should sound an alert, and some bark to let their people know they want to go out, come in, have dinner, or play.

However, obsessive, constant barking is usually a sign that something else is going on. Barking can be due to any number of factors, from sheer boredom to separation anxiety to an obsessive, nervous compulsion to guard the property

Dogs bark for different reasons. When you discover why your dog is barking, you can help correct his behavior.

Extreme Barkers

In extreme cases, you could have your dog debarked, which is better than euthanasia or eviction, but a questionable practice at best. This surgery cuts the vocal cords and while it does not eliminate barking, it lowers the volume and changes the sound somewhat. First try basic training methods like the ones described above and/or a bark collar before resorting to surgical alteration.

from anything that moves, be it a person walking down the street or a threatening onslaught of intruding snowflakes.

If your dog barks too much, it could annoy your neighbors, and you could even get evicted from a rental property. Barking dogs don't do well in certain environments, but let's assume your dog is there to stay. How do you address the problem?

Dogs bark for different reasons. If you have a barker, the first thing you need to ask yourself is: Why is he barking? If your neighbors complain that he is barking in the middle of the day while you are gone, try to find out a little more. He may be barking only when he hears the mail carrier and is warding off the approaching enemy, or he may bark each and every time he hears noises. He may be lonely and barking to make himself feel more confident. It may take a while to figure out, and you may have to observe your dog secretly, especially if he barks while you are gone. When you discover why he's barking, there are some things you can try to get him to stop the outta control noise.

* The best way to treat a barker is to build his confidence. It sounds so simple, right? The catch is that you have to give him that confidence, and it is only going to come through basic obedience, time, and attention.

* Leave the house as quietly as possible. Do not make a big fuss

Your Outta Control Adopted Dog

about saying goodbye to your puppy—it will only make him more anxious.

✳ If your dog seems lonely, leave a radio or television on when you leave. Noise from another room will bring him comfort and make him think that he is not alone.

✳ Be sure to exercise him before you crate or leave your dog. A well-exercised dog is far more likely to sleep the day away while you are gone.

✳ If your dog is busy, he won't bark. Leave him lots of toys and treats to play with while you are gone. A Crazy Ball by Nylabone® is an interactive toy that dispenses treat when your puppy rolls the ball around. Fill a paper bag with treats or give him a Rhino filled with cheese or peanut butter. These things should keep him occupied for long periods of time.

✳ Do not reinforce your dog's barking by trying to quiet him with petting or praise. If your puppy barks in your presence, ignore him and give him a treat when he's quiet.

All dogs want to be part of the family, and dogs that are left alone for long periods of time may develop a barking habit.

Practical Solutions to Outta Control Problems

* If your puppy or dog barks when the doorbell rings, silently put him in another room. Give him attention only when he's quiet, and then have him perform an obedience command, like sit or down.
* Teach him to speak on command. Although it sounds as if you are encouraging his barking, you are actually controlling it. He will learn that if he barks on command only, he will get praise and a treat, and it will reinforce his basic obedience.

Most important, remember that some dogs bark more than others, and general barking to alert you to the approach of people and dogs is perfectly normal. You can minimize it, but you can't totally eliminate it. Even the so-called "barkless" Basenji makes a lot of interesting noises.

Digging

Dogs dig for many reasons. Some dogs get all wound up and, not knowing what else to do with the excess energy, begin digging wildly. Some dogs, stuck all day in a yard with nothing to do, dig from pure boredom. Your terrier mix may dig out of instinct; true to his nature, he is in search of the rodents and varmints he was bred to control.

No matter what your situation, there are many steps you can take to live peacefully with your outta control digger.

* Daily exercise can help dogs that dig because of excess energy or boredom. When he can rely on daily exercise, he will begin to look forward to it.
* Begin a scheduled routine that promises a certain amount of mental and physical exercise. Dedicate at least ten minutes of that time to playing in the yard with your puppy, throwing a ball, or simply petting him as he sits contentedly next to you.
* Provide your dog with toys and bones when he's in your yard to

Your Outta Control Adopted Dog

Some dogs are natural diggers and need help redirecting their energy into more positive pursuits.

keep him occupied.

* Hold regular training sessions in the backyard. When you use your yard for training, you are reminding your pup that your rules apply there as well.

* Sometimes, your pup was born to dig—literally! You are fighting Mother Nature, and it may be a losing battle. If your terrier just needs to dig and nothing seems to work, you may find that you need to limit the area of his yard. Give him a sandbox or a corner of the yard in which he's allowed to dig. Fence off the places that you want him to stay away from, like your flower beds.

Jumping

Your dog is so happy to see you, and he shows his happiness by jumping all over you when you come in the room. It seems so cute that you may let it go or even encourage it by hugging and kissing him hello. However, little dogs become annoying and are too hard to catch; big dogs knock you down. Regardless of size, you have let the jumping slide, and you now have an outta control jumper who is putting muddy paw prints on your clothes and knocking little kids over. Just like preventing excessive barking, consistency is the key. Whatever your dog's age, start teaching him that jumping is not allowed—ever. Follow these steps to stop outta control jumping:

Teach your dog that jumping up on people is only allowed if they ask.

✱ Hold a treat in your hand as you open the door, and immediately distract your pup from jumping with the treat.

✱ Ask him to sit—another great form of restraint that will carry over to his adult life.

✱ As soon as he sits, tell him, "Good boy, good sit." Give him the treat and move past him. Give him another ten minutes to adjust to you being home before you give him the snuggles, hugs, and pats he deserves.

✱ Watch you voice—do not yell, do not be sweet. You do not want to startle him, nor do you want your voice to be so animated that it is even harder for him to contain his glee. Make sure your voice is monotone when you ask him to sit and offer the goody. He will learn quickly enough that if he is calm, he will get love from you a lot faster.

✱ For the chronic jumper, turn your back to him and go about your

Your Outta Control Adopted Dog

Guests and Goodies

Each time you have a guest come to the house, warn them ahead of time that you and your puppy are in training. Leave a baggie of goodies outside the door and ask them to have the dog sit and reward with a treat when they step inside the house. If everyone from your mom to the neighborhood paperboy expects and rewards your puppy's calm behavior, he will get the message very quickly.

business, ignoring him until he calms down. As soon as he is calm or sitting, praise him.

Jumping on Furniture

The best way to prevent this from happening is to never allow your dog on furniture in the first place—including your bed. In fairness to your dog, try not to send conflicting messages. It is unfair to let him on your

Consistency is the key to controlling problem behaviors. If you do not want your dog to jump on the furniture, then make it a household rule that is always obeyed.

Practical Solutions to Outta Control Problems

bed when you are feeling lonely and then expect him to understand that he's not welcome on your bed every night. If you are consistent with the rules, but your dog just can't seem to stay away from the chairs, you can try some of these ideas:

* Keep your dog crated or in a blocked-off room when you are not home. If your puppy is safely contained, you know he's not taking a nap on your couch.
* Provide your puppy with a soft bed or den of his own. You can give him a towel or a blanket that you have used, so he can still have your scent around to reassure him.
* If you have a dog who sneaks on to furniture when you're not looking, I recommend tin foil. Place a sheet of tin foil on your furniture cushions. The sound and feel of foil is very offensive to dogs, and they will get comfortable elsewhere.

Building a strong foundation between you and your adopted dog will create a lifelong bond between you.

Your Outta Control Adopted Dog

Relationship Maintenance

This kind of house rules training can mean the difference between the failure of the pet-human relationship and the success of helping your dog to become a well-behaved, lifelong companion that fulfills your every dream of what a pet dog should be. You can help your adopted dog's "outta control" behavior to evolve, slowly but surely, into a relationship that is meaningful and fulfilling for you and your entire family.

In the end, a successful adopted-dog/human relationship is all about maintenance. Think of your time as love. The more time you spend on your dog, the more effort you put in, the more you socialize, the more you train, the more you teach and enforce rules, and the more you simply enjoy each other, the better your relationship will be. Work with your dog, play with your dog, and spend time enjoying your adopted dog every single day. You can build a relationship that satisfies like no other: The relationship between human and dog, refined over thousands of years, and made perfect...by you!

Resources

Books

Adamson, Eve. *The Simple Guide to a Healthy Dog.*
(New Jersey: TFH, 2002.)

Allred, Alexandra Powe. *Teaching Basic Obedience: Train the Owner, Train the Dog.*
(New Jersey: TFH, 2001.)

Aloff, Brenda. *Positive Reinforcement: Training Dogs in the Real World.*
(New Jersey: TFH, 2001.)

Bauman, Diane. *Beyond Basic Dog Training,* new, updated edition.
(New York: Howell Book House, 1991.)

Becker, Dr. Marty. *The Healing Power of Pets.*
(New York: Hyperion, 2002.)

Bonham, Margaret. *The Simple Guide to Getting Active with Your Dog.*
(New Jersey: TFH, 2001.)

Coile, D. Caroline, Ph.D. *Encyclopedia of Dog Breeds.*
(New York: Barron's Educational Series, 1998.)

DePrisco, Andrew and Johnson, James. *Choosing a Dog for Life.*
(New Jersey, TFH, 1996.)

Dunbar, Dr. Ian. *Before You Get Your Puppy.*
(California: James & Kenneth Publishers, 2001.)

Kennedy, Stacy. *The Simple Guide to Puppies.* (New Jersey: TFH, 2000.)

Palika, Liz. *All Dogs Need Some Training.* (New York: Howell Book House, 1997.)

Pitcairn, Richard, DVM, and Susan Hubble Pitcairn. *Dr. Pitcairn's Guide to Natural Health for Dogs and Cats.* (Pennsylvania: Rodale Press, 1995.)

Pryor, Karen. *Don't Shoot the Dog! The New Art of Teaching and Training.* (New York: Bantam Books, 1984.)

Volhard, Jack and Wendy. *The Canine Good Citizen: Every Dog Can Be One.* (New York: Howell Book House, 1997.)

Volhard, Wendy and Kerry Brown, DVM. *Holistic Guide for a Healthy Dog,* second edition. (New York: Howell Book House, 2000.)

Wood, Deborah. *Help for Your Shy Dog.* (New York: Howell Book House, 1999.)

Organizations

American Kennel Club
Headquarters: 260 Madison Avenue
New York, NY 10016
Operations Center: 5580 Centerview Drive
Raleigh, NC 27606-3390
Customer Services:
Phone: 919-233-9767
www.akc.org

American Kennel Club's Canine Good Citizen:
www.akc.org/love/cgc/index.cfm

American Kennel Club's National Breed Club Rescue
www.akc.org/breeds/rescue.cfm

American Mixed Breed Obedience Association
179 Niblick Road #113
Paso Robles, CA 93446
Phone: 805-226-9275
www.amborusa.org

Animal Behavior Society
Indiana University
2611 East 10th Street #170
Bloomington, IN 47408-2603
Phone: 812-856-5541
www.animalbehavior.org

Association of Companion Animal Behavior Counselors
C/o American Instiute for Animal Science
PO Box 7922
Rego Park, NY 11374-7922
Phone: 877-229-5450
www.animalbehaviorcounselors.org

Association of Pet Dog Trainers
17000 Commerce Parkway Suite C
Mt. Laurel, NJ 08054
Phone: 1-800-PET-DOGS
www.apdt.com

The Canadian Kennel Club
89 Skyway Avenue, Suite 100
Etobicoke, Ontario, Canada M9W 6R4
Order Desk & Membership: 1-800-250-8040
www.ckc.ca

Humane Society of the United States
2100 L St., NW
Washington, DC 20037
Phone: 202-452-1100
www.hsus.org

The Kennel Club
1 Clarges Street
London, W1J 8AB
Phone: 087 0606 6750
www.the-kennel-club.org.uk

North American Dog Agility Council
11522 South Hwy 3
Cataldo, ID 83810
Phone: 973-252-9800
www.nadac.com

North Shore Animal League
750 Port Washington Blvd.
Port Washington, NY 11050
Phone: 516-883-7900
www.nsalamerica.org

Therapy Dogs International, Inc.
88 Bartley Road
Flanders, NJ 07836
Phone: 973-252-9800
www.tdi-dog.org

The United Kennel Club, Inc.
100 E. Kilgore Road
Kalamazoo, MI 49002-5584
Phone: 616-343-9020
www.ukcdogs.com

United States Dog Agility Association (USDAA)
PO Box 850955
Richardson, TX 75085-0955
Phone: 972-231-9700
888-AGILITY
www.usdaa.com

Index

Photos:

Isabelle Francais, Connie Isbell, Karen Taylor, John Tyson